Let the Whole Church Say Amen!

Let the Whole Church Say

Amen!

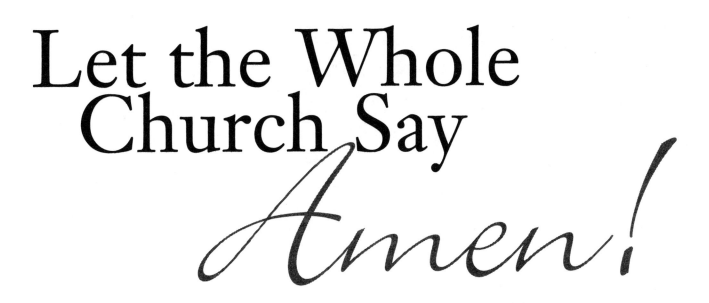

A Guide

for Those

Who Pray

in Public

LAURENCE HULL STOOKEY

Abingdon Press
Nashville

LET THE WHOLE CHURCH SAY AMEN!
A GUIDE FOR THOSE WHO PRAY IN PUBLIC

Library of Congress Cataloguing-in-Publication Data

Stookey, Laurence Hull, 1937–
    Let the whole church say Amen! : a guide for those who pray in public / Laurence Hull Stookey.
       p. cm.
    ISBN 0-687-090776
    1. Public worship. I. Title.

    BV15 .S76 2001
    264'.1—dc21

                                                                                            2001018173
ISBN 13:978-0-687-09077-8

12 13 14 15 16 17   17 16 15 14 13

MANUFACTURED IN THE UNITED STATES OF AMERICA

Throughout my three decades on the faculty of
Wesley Theological Seminary
my students have taught me much
about the discipline of public prayer.

To them I gratefully dedicate this book.

Acknowledgments

This book has been decades in the making. Knowingly or unwittingly, throughout that time hundreds of students have contributed to its formation through prayers they wrote and submitted to me in worship classes. Over the years I came to sense the need for such a book; since then several generations of seminarians have worked their way through various drafts, pointing out to me difficulties and making helpful suggestions. To them I have gratefully dedicated this volume.

The full faculty of Wesley Seminary has also read large sections of earlier drafts as a part of regular faculty study and discussion sessions in which we share our work-in-progress with colleagues and receive their critiques. I am appreciative of the affirmation given to me by my fellow faculty members and have tried to incorporate their insights into the text.

Much of the preparation of the final draft was done while I was also serving as Interim Pastor of Trinity and Town Point United Methodist Churches in Chesapeake City, Maryland. For their support and understanding of my sometimes compulsive work habits, I am grateful to members of those congregations. Especially I thank one parishioner there, Charmaine Lennox, who carefully read the manuscript from a layperson's vantage point and with an English teacher's eye for literary style.

Dr. Scott Haldeman, professor of liturgy at Chicago Theological Seminary, made many helpful suggestions while serving as my editor. To the entire Abingdon Press staff I extend deep gratitude.

Finally I necessarily remember a host of English teachers in high school and at Swarthmore College where I majored in literature. They infused me with a love of the mother tongue that has ever since made me choose words carefully and seek felicitous grammatical forms—particularly when these comprise praise and petition, confession and lament. I hope that this book will enable the church at prayer to use what the poet William Cowper called "this poor lisping, stammering tongue" to the fullness of its potential—as imperfect and inadequate as that will always be when offered up to God the Word Eternal.

Laurence Hull Stookey

Contents

	Introduction	11
Exercise 1	The Grandeur of God and Prayer as Pure Praise	13
Exercise 2	Learning a Basic Form for Brief Prayers	15
Exercise 3	Reviewing and Using the Basic Form	19
Exercise 4	The Collect Form with Modifications	23
Exercise 5	Learning to Pray with Vigorous Verbs	27
Interlude A	Patience and Persistence and Offerings to God	35
Exercise 6	On Heaping Up Empty Phrases	37
Exercise 7	Another Prayer Form: The Litany	43
Exercise 8	Achieving Variety and Breadth	49
Interlude B	To Write or Not to Write: Is *That* the Question?	53
Exercise 9	Corporate Prayers of Confession	59
Exercise 10	On the Holiness of God	65
Exercise 11	Praying to the God Who Is Present	73
Exercise 12	Praying to the Trinity	79
Interlude C	The Physical Aspects of Public Prayer	83
Exercise 13	Helping All to Feel Included	87
Exercise 14	The Lost Art of Lament	93
Exercise 15	The Pastoral Prayer and Related Forms	99
Exercise 16	Praying About Controversial Issues	105
Interlude D	The Sounds and Silence of Public Prayer	111
Exercise 17	Constructing a Thematic Prayer Based on Scripture	115
Exercise 18	Praying Outside the Church (Interreligious Settings)	121
Exercise 19	Writing Prayers for Unison Use	131
Exercise 20	Presiding at the Free Intercessions	135
Exercise 21	The Eucharistic Prayer	141
A Checklist	In Conclusion	147
Appendix 1	Selected Prayers and Their Use	149
Appendix 2	Praying in "The King James Way"	157
Appendix 3	Some Finer Points of Usage	163
	Notes	165

Introduction

To be asked to lead a group of Christ's people in prayer is a great honor and an equally great responsibility. Those who accept this leadership role are entrusted with a representative function: The prayer leader is expected to represent before God all of those who are present so that at the close of the prayer all can say with integrity the ancient word of assent: *Amen.*

Amen is a Hebrew word that has come down untranslated through Greek and Latin into English. Virtually every other language Christians speak has similarly made room for this untranslated term. Often said to mean "so be it," the amen expresses approval by others of what one person has said. (That is why it is a popular response within a sermon as well as at the end of a prayer.) If the prayer leader has not adequately spoken on behalf of those present, they cannot in good conscience say a hearty "amen" at the conclusion of the prayer.

As a leader of public prayer you are not being asked to utter your personal prayers in public, but rather to speak on behalf of the whole church. Personal prayers may include matters too specific for public use. When spoken in public, some things you properly pray for at home constitute a breach of confidence or an airing of matters considered by many to be too personal for comfort. For example, in private you properly confess sins that you have committed. In public you need to make much more general statements of confession, so that these apply to all present, not to you alone. At home you may pray for individuals whose needs are known to you but who do not want those needs announced widely. In public you are required to pray in more general terms, in order not to betray confidences and thus break the bond of trust. Therefore leadership in public prayer implies careful preparation and the observance of certain principles of expression that allow all present to feel they have been adequately and accurately represented before God. That is what this book is all about.

Some of you who read these pages will be entrusted with public prayer because you are volunteer (unpaid) leaders within a congregation. Perhaps you have been elected to chair a board or committee, and offering prayer at the beginning or end of each meeting is an expected part of your leadership role. Or you may have a designated title of a more general nature such as deacon, lay speaker, lay leader, or church school superintendent. Other readers will have more professional (salaried) roles as pastors, directors of Christian education, or congregational program coordinators.

It is likely that those who use this manual will also be at various stages within similar leadership roles. Some of you may be volunteer leaders fresh to the task, and you may understandably face the prospect of praying in public with some anxiety. Others of you, whether laity or clergy, may feel much more comfortable because of having led in public prayer for many years, but now perhaps you sense that you have fallen into a rut, saying the same things time after time until your prayers are predictable. So you may take this book in hand as a form of remedial action. Still others who use this manual may be students enrolled in a theological seminary or other formal program, who have been assigned this book as part of a course requirement.

As a way of addressing all of you, I shall present material in stages, almost as in the teaching of a foreign language. I will not assume that you have any formal training in theology, and I hope those who have such preparation will not feel the approach is "beneath" them. If you already have some experience in public prayer, you may be tempted to hurry on past the opening exercises in this book in order to get to the more challenging portions quickly. I suggest you not do that, as later exercises will ask you to come back to the first sets of exercises and see what changes you would make in your writing in light of further discussion and learning. Please complete each written exercise in turn.

Yes, you will here be asked to write out prayers. This does not necessarily mean either (a) that you must always write your public prayers, or (b) that having written them you should "read" them from a manuscript. Often you will be called upon to pray without warning; hence no document can be prepared in advance. In some settings, using a written prayer is frowned upon as being unauthentic or insincere. Furthermore, some people can pray aloud from a manuscript in a way that sounds fresh and spontaneous. But those who lack this ability are better advised to write a manuscript as a way of clarifying and organizing their thoughts, but then to put the manuscript aside and not use it at all in public, or to reduce it to a set of reminders rather than a word-for-word document.

Writing is employed here as an important part of self-discipline and analysis. This is indeed a workbook, and adequate space is provided for you to write out whatever is being assigned in the exercises. If you are enrolled in a formal curriculum, your instructor will divide the exercises into assignments of appropriate length. If you are using this book on your own, I strongly urge you not to attempt too much in one sitting. It is better to work in short segments every two or three days than to try to complete a large chunk of work once every week or ten days. Instead, follow a schedule such as might be appropriate in learning a language. Interspersed among the exercises are "interludes"—sections that give you material to ponder without any written exercise attached. You may wish to read an interlude on the same day that you do an exercise, or you may find it more helpful to study the interlude apart from any written assignment that day.

Before starting your work on each exercise, I urge you to engage in a brief prayer of petition and meditation concerning your task. Prayer should be itself a preparation for learning to pray more adequately. Something like this is appropriate before you begin each work session:

Gracious God,
    you have called your people together
        to worship and serve your world
            through the ministry of your church.
    You have given me the privilege of leading your people in prayer
        from time to time.
    Open my heart and mind to ways of praying
        that enable all who gather with me on such occasions
            to feel that I have represented them well in your presence.
    Grant this for the sake of Jesus Christ who taught his disciples to pray:

Our Father in heaven, hallowed be your name;
your kingdom come, your will be done on earth as in heaven.
Give us today our daily bread.
Forgive us our sins
    as we forgive those who sin against us.
Save us from the time of trial and deliver us from evil.
For the kingdom, the power, and the glory are yours,
    now and for ever. Amen.

You may be more comfortable using a traditional translation of the Lord's Prayer (with "art" and "thy") rather than the contemporary ecumenical version I have provided above. But in this manual we will be addressing God largely in the language patterns of the twenty-first century, not the sixteenth. Therefore the ecumenical translation of the Lord's Prayer consistent with contemporary conversation is provided here, and I recommend it heartily for your use, at least on occasion.

The heading of each exercise suggests also a reading from Scripture that either is a prayer (such as a Psalm) or a biblical teaching related to our understanding of prayer. These are intended both to stimulate your thinking and to remind you of the form of biblical prayer

Now, when you are ready, please move on to exercise 1.

Exercise 1

The Grandeur of God and Prayer as Pure Praise

Read Revelation 4:6b-11 and 7:9-12.

Please begin your work today by reading the suggested passages from the Revelation and offering personal prayer such as that recommended at the close of the introduction. Then proceed to what follows below.

Often we think of prayer as primarily a way of asking God for something. Certainly requests for ourselves or for others are an important part of prayer. But before and beyond that, there is prayer that asks for nothing whatsoever, but simply praises the grandeur and goodness of God. God is worthy of thanksgiving and honor. Such prayer without petition is deeply rooted in the tradition of Jewish and Christian piety. Consider, for example, Psalm 8; it consists of nine verses addressed to God, without a single request being made. The same is true of the thirteen verses of Psalm 65. Read and meditate on both of these Psalms.

Then look again at the passages from the Revelation and note that these prayers to God include no requests. Of course, the setting of the passage is heaven. There communication with God is direct, and the trials and difficulties present on earth are absent; hence there is less reason for petition.

But prayer as pure praise is a fine starting place for our own earth-bound journey toward heaven. So here is your first assignment: On the lines provided, write a prayer of pure praise. As you proceed, check to be certain you have not inserted any requests into your act of thanksgiving and adoration.

_____

_____

_____

_____

_____

_____

_____

_____

_____

When you have finished, again read the passages from the Revelation and Psalms 8 and 65. Does the prayer you have constructed seem as free of requests as those biblical prayers?

Exercise 2

Learning a Basic Form for Brief Prayers

Read Romans 15:5-6, 2 Corinthians 1:3-7, and 1 Thessalonians 5:23-24.

In exercise 1, I gave you no instruction concerning the form your prayer of pure praise might take—no suggestions about content or order or length. Perhaps that made you uneasy; in fact, I hope it did. For we human beings are generally much more comfortable with some guidance and pattern than we are without. Perhaps this is one of the indications that we have been created in the image and likeness of God. For God seems to like order. Before creation, everything was "formless," and God took on the task of organizing it all (see Genesis 1:2). And Paul advises us that all things should be done decently and in order, for God is not a God of disorder (1 Cor. 14:40, 33). So now we are going to explore a particular form many prayers take. Mastery of this form and its variations can put you at ease in specific situations. And, yes, in these prayers we will be making requests of God.

Let's suppose that you are being called upon to offer a prayer at the beginning of a rather routine meeting of church business. You realize that the agenda for this session of a board or major committee is a full one and that therefore your prayer should be brief. Here are steps you can follow.

1. Begin your preparation by thinking of a central petition to God. On such an occasion this might be a request for wisdom and goodwill in decision making. For example:

> *By the power of your Holy Spirit*
>   *open our minds to your wisdom*
>   *and our hearts to your love*
>   *throughout our deliberations.*

2. That done, next think of a reason for making this request. What do you hope will be the outcome if your request is granted? This purpose is going to be attached to the petition, and hence it begins with the word *that*. The whole thing may look like this:

> *By the power of your Holy Spirit*
>   *open our minds to your wisdom*
>   *and our hearts to your love*
>   *throughout our deliberations,*
> *that we may act wisely for the good*
>   *of our church and community.*

If this meeting has to do primarily with the missionary or evangelistic work of the congregation, the purpose instead may be:

15

that the good news of your grace
    may be effectively spread to others and embraced by them.

If this is a meeting concerned largely with the allocation of church funds, an alternative purpose may be

that we may be good stewards
    of all that you have entrusted to us.

If the meeting portends a "church fight" over a controversial issued, this purpose may be appropriate:

that we may seek your will above our own and may with one heart carry out
    your work in this place.

Any one of these four purposes can fit nicely with the request given above. But although there is no "one right way" to state the purpose of the request, on specific occasions there may be a very wrong way to go about it. What you cannot do if all present are going to say the amen is state a purpose such as this when a very controversial proposal is under consideration:

that we may approve the carefully prepared proposal before us without amendment or dissension
    in fulfillment of your will for our church.

That language is too "loaded." It reveals too fully your own personal view of the pending legislation. As a leader of prayer, you are being trusted to represent the whole body, not to make a partisan speech on behalf of one side of a hotly debated proposal. No matter how wise you yourself may think the proposal in question to be, in prayer you are to represent the whole body—not simply those whom you expect to vote with you. Only in this way can everyone say "amen" with a good conscience. Always keep in mind that your goal is to enable the whole church to say "amen" at the close of your prayer.

3. Whatever your purpose for making the request, next think of something in the nature of God that allows or even encourages you to present this petition and purpose. (Although you may decide on this only after having thought of the petition and purpose, this phrase will come at the beginning of the prayer, not at the end.) Since this is a church meeting, the undergirding assumption may well be that God has established the church and has given to us the responsibility of carrying out its day-to-day functioning. Hence we may approach God remembering that
You have created the church and entrusted to us the task of carrying out its work in this place.

4. With an underlying assumption, a petition, and a purpose behind the petition, now we have everything necessary for this brief prayer except a beginning and an ending. Let's keep it simple by addressing the Almighty simply as "O God." And the most direct and universal way in which Christians close their prayers is "through Jesus Christ our Lord." Now the full prayer reads as follows:

O God,
you have created the church and entrusted to us
    the task of carrying out its work in this place.
By the power of your Holy Spirit
    open our minds to your wisdom
    and our hearts to your love throughout our deliberations,
that we may act wisely for the good of our church and community;*
through Jesus Christ our Lord.

*Here any of the other three purposes discussed above could be used instead.

To this prayer those present should be able to add their hearty amen.

Note that this prayer consists of five parts (each beginning a new line of type above, to assist you in seeing the form). The parts have names, as follows:

1. Address (or salutation)	*O God,*
2. Attribution (or ascription)	*you have created . . . in this place.*
3. Petition	*By the power . . . our deliberations,*
4. Purpose	*that we may . . . church and community;*
5. Closing	*through Jesus Christ our Lord.*

It will help you in the future if you now commit the names of these five parts to memory in order. Repeat to yourself a number of times: "address, attribution, petition, purpose, closing."

Now suppose that you are rather suddenly called upon to give a prayer before a meal. It would be kinder of people to ask you well ahead of time whether you will ask the table blessing. But particularly if you are a member of the clergy, often those who make the request will not always be so thoughtful; they will assume that you are chock-full of prayers on any subject, and that these can come rolling out at a moment's notice. If you have mastered the form used above, you will be able to offer prayers on short notice with less anxiety and greater facility without beating around the bush while trying to think of what to say. That will be particularly appreciated when people are very hungry and the mashed potatoes and gravy are getting cold!

So begin mentally by getting in hand a petition such as this:
Strengthen us with this food prepared for our benefit,
Then add a purpose:
that we may more adequately do your work in the world
    and share your bounty with others;
Precede this with an attribution. Often an attribution is based on Scripture. Perhaps you happen to know Isaiah 55:10, which mentions God's action of "giving seed to the sower and bread to the eater." (The more Scripture you know, the more readily you will find phrases of attribution.) This text can readily be made into an attribution:
You give seed to those who sow and bread to those who eat.
Now the heart of the prayer is completed. Only an opening and closing need to be supplied. Since the prayer deals with God's goodness and bounty, an appropriate yet simple address is:
Gracious God,
Because Jesus told us that he is himself the bread of life, the brief closing used in the prayer for a business meeting ("through Jesus Christ our Lord") may be elaborated a bit: *through Jesus Christ, who is the Bread of Life.*
Now the prayer looks like this:

Gracious God:
you give seed to those who sow and bread to those who eat.
Strengthen us with this food prepared for our benefit,
that we may more adequately do your work in the world
    and share your bounty with others;
through Jesus Christ, who is the Bread of Life.

The prayer is concise as the occasion demands, yet it contains a great deal of substance. It makes important affirmations about God and about the work God has given us to do.

At first it will seem a bit odd to have to build the prayer from the inside out by starting with a petition, adding a purpose to the back end of it and an attribution to the front end, and then appending an address and a closing. As you master this five-part form, you will be able to start at the beginning and work your way through in 1, 2, 3, 4, 5 order rather than the 3, 4, 2, 1, 5 order we have used in constructing these two prayers. Even so, particularly if a prayer needs to be brief (as it must be, for example, in the emergency ward of a hospital), you first need to think about the heart of the matter: What are we asking of God? That is always the central issue. Then come the supporting questions: Why are we asking for this? *and* What about the God we worship makes this an appropriate request?

In a sense parts 2 and 4 (the attribution and the purpose) are protective layers around the petition; these ensure that the prayer expresses Christian sentiment, not selfish desire. If we cannot think of a defensible purpose or cannot find anything in the nature of God that warrants our petition, we may need to reexamine our request. Why, for example, would we offer a petition asking God to make our congregation the largest church in town? Is the fact that we like to be on the "winning team" reason enough? Upon close examination that hardly seems a worthy purpose. And what about the nature of God? Do we serve a God who is predictably on the side of the majority? (There is plenty of evidence in Scripture that God is often on the side of the few rather than of the many. See, for example, the story of Gideon in Judges 7:2-23 and Mary's Magnificat in Luke 1:46-55.) If we cannot come up with a better purpose or attribution than these, perhaps our desire to belong to the biggest congregation in town is a self-centered human wish for prestige rather than a legitimate Christian petition. Forcing ourselves to look carefully at the purpose and the attribution can alert us to requests that we can hardly offer "through Jesus Christ."

If your religious inclinations make you a bit suspicious of the form I have just set forth, look closely with me at the three biblical passages I suggested for reading at the beginning of this exercise. In each of these, Paul gives us the raw material for a five-part prayer:

Romans 15:5-6
May the God of steadfastness and encouragement grant you to live in harmony with one another, in accordance with Christ Jesus, so that together you may with one voice glorify the God and Father of our Lord Jesus Christ.

> *Gracious God,*
> *the source of steadfastness and encouragement:*
> *Enable us to live in harmony with one another,*
> *that we may with one voice glorify you,*
> *in accordance with Christ Jesus, through whom we pray.*

2 Corinthians 1:3-4
Blessed be the God and Father of our Lord Jesus Christ, the Father of mercies and the God of all consolation, who consoles us in all our affliction, so that we may be able to console those who are in any affliction with the consolation with which we ourselves are consoled by God.

> *Blessed God,*
> *from you comes all mercy and consolation.*
> *Console us in all our affliction,*
> *that we may be able likewise to console those who are in any affliction;*
> *through Jesus Christ our Lord.*

1 Thessalonians 5:23-24
May the God of peace himself sanctify you entirely; and may your spirit and soul and body be kept sound and blameless at the coming of our Lord Jesus Christ. The one who calls you is faithful, and he will do this.

> *O God of peace:*
> *You have called us and you are faithful.*
> *Sanctify us entirely,*
> *that our spirits, souls, and bodies may be kept sound and blameless*
>   *at the coming of the One through whom we pray,*
> *our Lord Jesus Christ.*

Far from being alien to biblical expression and piety, this simple and ancient five-part structure of prayer can aid us greatly in learning to pray the Scriptures. Now again, recite the five parts: address, attribution, petition, purpose, closing. Say these words several times to fix them in your memory.

Exercise 3

Reviewing and Using the Basic Form

Read Philippians 4:4-9.

After pondering the biblical passage, remember to engage in a period of prayer.
Then recall the form for a brief prayer studied in exercise 2. Name the five parts in order. If you cannot, go back and review the list. Repeat these five parts until you have them firmly memorized.

This five-part order constitutes one of the most ancient and prevalent ways in which Christians have formed short prayers. The form is called a *collect*, with the accent on the first syllable: *COL-lect* (not the more usual *col-LECT*). The English language has a number of words that emphasize the second syllable when the word is a verb, but the first syllable when the word is a noun. For example: "The committee's secretary was asked to *re-CORD* the motion, so that it would be available at a later time in the printed *REC-ord*." Or again, "The prospective home owner agreed to *con-TRACT* a financial arrangement with the builder; their agreement was set forth in a signed *CON-tract*." *Collect* is another of those English words. The origins of the noun are lost in history, but certainly this form of prayer collects into a very concise form a great deal of faith and meaning. That may be how the noun came into being. In any event, thousands of collects have been written across the centuries, and many are preserved for our use. Some denominations have a prescribed collect for every Sunday and for every other major worship occasion in the Christian year.

One of the best-known prayers in English is "The Collect for Purity," preserved in the communion liturgies of many Protestant denominations. It is given below in both its traditional and contemporary forms. Notice its five parts:

Traditional

1. Almighty God,
2. unto whom all hearts are open, all desires known,
   and from whom no secrets are hid:
3. Cleanse the thoughts of our hearts,
   by the inspiration of thy Holy Spirit,
4. that we may perfectly love thee
   and worthily magnify thy holy name;
5. through Christ our Lord.

Contemporary

1. Almighty God,
2. to you all hearts are open, all desires known,
   and from you no secrets are hidden.
3. Cleanse the thoughts of our hearts
   by the inspiration of your Holy Spirit,
4. that we may perfectly love you
   and worthily magnify your holy name;
5. through Christ our Lord.

If you observe the wording carefully, you will note that in part 5 the prayer is offered through "Christ our Lord" rather than through the more usual "Jesus Christ our Lord." This is an acceptable variation, of the kind we will discuss more fully when we look further at the collect form in exercise 4.

Tradition attributes the Collect for Purity to Alcuin, an English cleric who was a chief advisor to the Emperor Charlemagne, though there is some reason to believe that before his death in 804 Alcuin simply preserved for us a prayer that began to be used centuries earlier.

Now you are ready to write a collect of your own. Note well that normally a collect has only one subject. Perhaps you will want to use one of the subjects already discussed—an opening prayer for a church meeting or a table grace. But you may well have some other occasion or need in mind: a collect with a person facing surgery; for the hungry and homeless; for those who mourn; for world peace; and so on.

Before beginning to construct the prayer in your mind, pray for God's direction and aid. Then select a subject and proceed.

Write the subject on the first line below. Then fill in the five parts as is most natural for you. (You may write them down in the 3, 4, 2, 1, 5 order; or you may simply work through that order in your mind and then put your thoughts on paper in 1, 2, 3, 4, 5 order. It doesn't matter, so long as you maintain the single subject throughout the prayer.)

Subject: _____

1. Address

_____

_____

2. Attribution

_____

_____

3. Petition

_____

_____

4. Purpose

_____

_____

5. Closing

_____

When you are finished, look over your work carefully. Are all parts of the prayer closely related to the subject you chose? A good collect should **not** look like this:

Creator God,
you have bought our redemption on the cross.
Provide for the needs of all who are hungry and homeless,
that Christian missionaries may spread your gospel throughout the world;
through Jesus Christ, the Prince of Peace.

Although this prayer has the usual five parts, the person who wrote it could not decide which of five subjects to pursue: creation, redemption, hunger and homelessness, the missionary effort, or peace. So be certain you have one focus throughout your prayer. Multiple subjects will be quite appropriate in the longer prayers you will learn to create later in this manual; but the collect lends itself only to one thing at a time.

Ask a number of questions about the form of your prayer:

Is the address brief? If it contains more than three or four words, it may be more than an address.

Does the attribution state something about the nature of God, preferably an attribute that can be clearly supported from scripture?

Is the petition clear and precise? Does it begin with a vigorous verb? (More on that in future exercises.)

Does the purpose begin with the word *that* or the phrase *so that*? If not, likely it is not a purpose.

Does the closing begin with the word *through* and make mention of Jesus?

(This is not the only possible form of closing, but for now we will pretend that it is and will deal with other options as we go along.)

In light of these questions, you may now want to make changes or revisions to your first draft.

In case you are writing your collect to be printed out in a Sunday service folder, for example, you may be wondering about proper punctuation. As the collect form dictates the parts of the prayer, so in large measure it also prescribes punctuation. There are variations, but the most usual pattern is this:

Address	followed by a comma	
Attribution	followed by a period	(sometimes by a colon)
Petition	followed by a comma	
Purpose	followed by a semicolon	(sometimes by a comma)
Closing	followed by a period	

You really need not worry about this if you are preparing collects to be said aloud by one person. But if you are printing them for unison use, you may want to memorize this pattern:

comma
period
comma
semicolon
period

Note that this is the punctuation used for the contemporary form of the Collect for Purity above. Of course there may be punctuation within each of the five parts as well as at the end of each part; such internal punctuation is determined by the logic of the grammatical construction used within that particular section.

The Collect Form with Modifications

Read Luke 11:5-13.

The collect form you have just learned does not always contain all five parts. Learning its variations will provide you with a greater sense of freedom in constructing collects, but it will also help in short prayers of various kinds, even those that do not follow the collect form.

Except in a prayer that is only praise and thanksgiving or only confession without any appeal for forgiveness, there will always be a petition (part 3). Except in rare cases, a prayer will always have an address (part 1) and some form of closing (part 5). Therefore the only dispensable parts in the collect form are the attribution (part 2) and the purpose (part 4). Usually no more than one of these two optional parts will be missing from any prayer that qualifies as a collect in form.

Read carefully this prayer and note which part is missing:

Almighty and ever-living God,
increase in us your gift of faith,
that, forsaking what lies behind
and reaching out to what is before,
we may run the way of your commandments
and win the crown of everlasting joy;
through Jesus Christ our Lord,
who lives and reigns with you and the Holy Spirit,
one God, forever and ever.[1]

Did you identify what is absent? There is here no attribution. The prayer moves directly from the address to God to the verb of petition ("increase"). Several other things to note:

(a) The petition is quite brief (*"increase in us the gift of faith"*), but the purpose is rather long (*"that, forsaking what lies behind and reaching out to what is before, we may run the way of your commandments and win the crown of everlasting joy"*). Not only is this disparity in length acceptable, but it can provide a certain variety of pace.

(b) There is a double purpose: *"that we may run"* and (that we may) *"win."*

(c) This prayer relies heavily upon scripture, and thus enables us to pray the Bible: *"Forsaking what lies behind and reaching to what is before"* is based on Philippians 3:13. *"We may run the way of your commandments"* calls to mind several verses that use the metaphor of a race: 1 Corinthians 9:24; Philippians 2:16; and Hebrews 12:1. *"Win the crown of everlasting joy"* alludes to 2 Timothy 4:8; James 1:12; 1 Peter 5:4; and the Revelation 2:10.

(d) Observe the elaborated ending. The simple *"through Jesus Christ our Lord"* is here expanded into a full trinitarian closing. In some Christian traditions the more elaborated trinitarian closing is used frequently, or even almost exclusively; other denominations prefer in most instances the brevity of *"through Jesus Christ our Lord."* Become familiar with the preferences of your own church body.

Now let's look at another modified collect form that lacks an attribution:

Lord God, so rule and govern our hearts and minds by your Holy Spirit that, always keeping in mind the end of all things and the day of judgment, we may be stirred up to holiness of life here and may live with you forever in the world to come, through your Son, Jesus Christ our Lord.[2]

Note that in addition to having no attribution, there is again a double purpose: (1) "*that . . . we may be stirred up to holiness of life,*" and (2) (that we) "*may live with you forever in the world to come.*" It is not uncommon to have a double purpose or a double petition. Occasionally there is even both a double petition and a double purpose. Again, variety is useful.

Sometimes in a collect that lacks an attribution, the prayer begins with the verb of request and then inserts the address into the midst of the petition, as follows:

Pour out upon us, O Lord, the spirit to think and do what is right, that we, who cannot even exist without you, may have the strength to live according to your will; through your Son, Jesus Christ our Lord.[3]

These types of variations in which the attribution is deleted keep a simple five-part form from becoming too routine and predictable.

Notice that the collect just quoted could have been written in the usual five parts, as follows, but it would sound less original:

O Lord,
without you we cannot even exist.
Pour out upon us the spirit to think and do what is right,
that we may have the strength to live according to your will;
through your Son, Jesus Christ our Lord.

While some modified collects lack an attribution, others have no stated purpose:

Lord God, whose blessed Son our Savior gave his body to be whipped and his face to be spit upon: Give us grace to accept joyfully the sufferings of the present time, confident of the glory that shall be revealed; through Jesus Christ your Son our Lord, who lives and reigns with you and the Holy Spirit, one God, for ever and ever.[4]

Note this: The phrase "*that shall be revealed*" is not a purpose. It is a modifying phrase attached to the word *glory*. Not every *that* signals the beginning of a statement of purpose. The prayer could be recast in this way in order to have a stated purpose:

Lord God,
whose blessed Son our Savior gave his body to be whipped and his face to be spit upon:
Give us grace to accept joyfully the sufferings of the present time,
that we may be confident of the glory that shall be revealed;
through, etc.

But the writer of this prayer did not see confidence to be a **result** of suffering, but that which is already present and enables us to endure suffering. So rewriting this collect to make it follow the five part form alters the meaning of the author.

Consider this collect:

Remember, O Lord, what you have wrought in us and not what we deserve; and, as you have called us to your service, make us worthy of our calling; through Jesus Christ our Lord, who lives and reigns with you and the Holy Spirit, one God, now and for ever.[5]

In this instance:

(a) The prayer begins with the first petition (*Remember . . .*); the address (*O Lord*) is inserted into it.

(b) There is a double petition; (1) "*remember what you have wrought in us and not what we deserve*"; and (2) "*make us worthy of our calling.*" ("*As you have called us to your service*" modifies the second petition. The meaning of the phrase is clearer if we restate it this way: "*Inasmuch as you have . . .* ")

(c) There is neither an attribution nor a purpose. As noted earlier, the deletion of both is rare—but not unknown.

The point to all of this? If writing a prayer of five parts at first seems to you to be wooden and artificial, there is much greater freedom within the form than appears initially. My intention is not that you should at this stage master all of the possible variations; rather, I hope you can see that the form may help you to be creative—as well as saving you from becoming tongue-tied when you are called upon without warning to offer a public prayer.

Now try to use the collect form to put into prayer a favorite passage of Scripture. First think of a biblical passage you would like to pray. It may be something very familiar (John 3:16 or Psalm 23:1-3), or it may be something less well known. You may construct your prayer in five parts, or you may decide to delete the attribution or the purpose.

Biblical passage _____

1. Address

_____

2. Attribution

_____

_____

3. Petition

_____

_____

4. Purpose

_____

_____

5. Closing

_____

Look over your work carefully. Do you have the same number of parts that you intended to use? Are the attribution, petition, and purpose (if you used all three) drawn from the biblical passage you chose?

There is no one correct way to complete this exercise. A collect based on John 3:16 might look somewhat like any one of the three following forms. First, the standard five-part form:

> *1. Gracious God,*
> *2. you have loved the world so much as to send to us your only Son.*
> *3. Enable us to believe in him with true faith,*
> *4. that we may not perish but have eternal life;*
> *5. through this same Jesus Christ our Savior.*

Alternatively, the prayer can be written without an attribution, but with the same material found therein embodied in the petition:

> *1. Gracious God,*
> *3. enable us to believe in your only Son, whom you have sent into the world you love,*
> *4. that we may not perish but have eternal life;*
> *5. through this same Jesus Christ our Savior.*

Another variation omits the purpose, yet still includes the essentials of the familiar verse from John:

> *1. Gracious God,*
> *2. you have loved the world so much as to send to us your only Son.*
> *3. Enable us not to perish but to have eternal life by believing in him;*
> *5. through this same Jesus Christ our Savior.*

Note: In earlier times, if Jesus was mentioned in parts 2, 3, or 4 (whether by name or merely by a readily recognized title such as "only Son"), it was deemed necessary in part 5 to use the phrase "the same," so everyone would clearly understand the unity of both the prayer and the Trinity. This is no longer a rigid rule, but in the above instance it seemed to me that using "this same" causes the prayer to read more smoothly.

You may now want to go back to the prayer you just wrote and make some modifications in it. Then you may wish to write out several collects for various purposes. Finally, think of a situation in which you may unexpectedly be called upon to pray; without the use of writing instrument or paper, try saying a prayer appropriate to the occasion, using the collect form or any of its variations.

For the sake of variety, we are now going to turn to a longer kind of prayer that does not follow any standard form. Even so, I think you will see how the elements of the collect turn up in one way or another in longer prayers.

Learning to Pray with Vigorous Verbs

Read Matthew 6:9-13.

A good story, well told, marches along on sturdy verbs. So also does a good prayer. When the disciples of Jesus asked him to teach them how to pray, he provided a prayer that used vigorous verbs as a model for them to follow when making petitions to God:

Give	(us today our daily bread.)
Forgive	(us our sins, as we forgive those who sin against us.)
Save	(us from the time of trial.)
Deliver	(us from evil.)

Notice what Jesus did not say:

Let us today find our daily bread.
We hope that we may be forgiven, as we forgive those who sin against us.
Be with us in the time of trial.
May we escape evil.

Some Christians are troubled by prayers that are as direct as the first set of petitions. "Do we dare to pray that way?" they ask. "It seems as if we are ordering God around." Yet it is no less an authority than Jesus who gives us permission to be so bold. Nor did he invent the idea. The Hebrew Scriptures are filled with vigorous verbs of prayer:

Give ear, O Shepherd of Israel,
    you who lead Joseph like a flock!
You who are enthroned upon the cherubim, *shine forth*
    before Ephraim and Benjamin and Manasseh.
Stir up your might,
and *come to save* us
Restore us, O God.

(Psalm 80:1-3*a*, emphasis added)

God is not some stranger whom we must approach timidly. We have the liberty as children of God to say boldly what we have in our hearts, trusting that God will sift the wheat from the chaff of our prayers.

Some verbs of prayer are particularly anemic. Chief among these is the very popular *be with* petition. Not only is this weak because it says little, but it contravenes the promises of the Christ (highlighted in the following verses):

For where two or three are gathered in my name, *I am there* among them (Matt. 18:20).

I am with you always to the end of the age (Matt. 28:20).

Further, a crucial title of Jesus is *Emmanuel,* a Hebrew term meaning "God is with us" (Matt. 1:23). To suggest instead that as Christian people we need to ask God to "be with" us is regrettable at best. Fortunately most people who use this phrase in prayer intend no heresy but simply neglect to come up with a better verb. Charles Wesley was thinking more clearly and precisely about the matter of the presence of God with us at all times when he wrote:

Jesus, we look to thee,
Thy promised presence claim;
Thou in the midst of us shalt be,
Assembled in thy name.
Present we know thou art,
But O thyself reveal!
Now, Lord, let every bounding heart
The mighty comfort feel.[6]

Christ's promise, "Remember, I am with you always, to the end of the age," is not to be taken lightly (Matt. 28:20). Nor is the promise that "where two or three are gathered in my name, I am there among them" to be ignored (Matt. 18:20). If Christ is with us in fulfillment of these promises, we need not pray "be with us." At best, this is an unneeded petition, and at worst it may seem to connate a deep lack of faith in that which we have been promised.

Therefore when a sufferer is unsure of the presence of God, the appropriate petition is not "Be with *Name*" but "Reveal to *Name* the certainty of your constant, comforting presence." As Christians, we confidently believe that God promises always to be present among us; Charles Wesley understood that when it seems otherwise, it is our perception that needs to be corrected, not God's location.

Another verb that often says little is *bless*. Occasionally it is exactly the right verb of petition. We appropriately ask God at the Eucharist to "bless these gifts of bread and wine." But in other instances *bless* is a rather weak substitute for *strengthen* (the weak), *encourage* (those who see no hope), *guide* (all who are confused), *heal* (the sick), and similarly hardy verbs.

The phrases *may we* and *let us* are also anemic in the context of prayer. In fact, they are phrases addressed not so much to God as to the congregation. They are words of exhortation, not petition. As such, they tend to convey a "bootstrap" theology: All we have to do to get the answer to our prayers is work harder, think more positively, exert more faith. Taken to the extreme, such verbiage seems to make God unnecessary. "Let *us* do what is called for;" "May *we* work more diligently and be more faithful." And suddenly prayers of petition for divine help evaporate into the thin air of psychological manipulation and good works. God's role becomes unclear and seemingly unnecessary.

Because biblical faith never in this way dispenses with God's work, the prayers of the Bible are filled with vigorous verbs, as we have noted in both the Lord's Prayer and Psalm 80; and those passages are merely short, representative examples of the much larger body of biblical prayer, which is filled with direct appeals to God, couched in a sturdy vocabulary of petition.

Pause now and spend ten or fifteen minutes mentally searching for verbs of prayer that are vigorous. Some verbs at first may seem too negative to include on your list, but coupled with the right nouns even these may be very appropriate. For example, you may be tempted to cast aside as inappropriate verbs such as *pursue* or *defeat*. But at times such words say precisely what is fitting: "*Pursue* the forces of sin and death and *defeat* them."

Record your verbs below.

When you have finished making your list, look over it carefully and ask: "How often recently in prayer have I used such words? How can I become more comfortable with this vocabulary; and how can I more fully incorporate it into my prayers, both private and public?"

Consider as a model of boldness this prayer from the fourth-century Christian, Basil of Caesarea:

Remember, O Lord, this congregation present, and those who are absent with good cause.
Have mercy upon them and upon us, according to the multitude of your loving kindness.
Fill their garners with good things.
Preserve their marriages in peace and love.
Take care of their little ones;
lead their youth;
give strength to the aged.
Comfort the timid and afraid.
Bring home the scattered.
Restore those who have erred.
And unite them all in your holy catholic and apostolic church.
Heal those who are vexed with unclean spirits.
Go with all traveling by sea or by land.

Protect the widow;
shelter the orphans.
Deliver . . . those who work in mines, and those in exile;
   those in distress or poverty, or any kind of trouble.
Remember all who stand in need of your pity:
   those that love us; those that hate us;
   those who desire our prayers, unworthy though we be to offer them to you.
Remember, O Lord, all of your people, and pour upon them in abundance
   your goodness, granting all their prayers unto salvation.
All those whom we have not remembered through ignorance or forgetfulness
   or through the multitude of their names,
    do yourself call to mind, O God;
   for you know the name and age of each, even from our mother's womb.
For you, O Lord, are
   the helper of the helpless;
   the hope of the hopeless;
   the savior of the tempest-tossed;
   the harbor of the voyager; and
   and the physician of the sick.
Be all things to all people.
For you know them all, their petitions, their dwellings, and their minds.[7]

This prayer is wonderfully strong and admirably comprehensive, thereby reflecting and giving testimony to the faith of the whole church; despite its length, it does not suffer from a repetition or redundancy that wearies the worshiper. Rather, it moves along rapidly on a majestic procession of verbs addressed to God: "Remember, have (mercy), fill, preserve, take, lead, give, comfort, bring, restore, unite, heal, go with, protect, shelter, deliver. . . ." The congregation that prays in this manner witnesses far more amply to the nature of Christian faith than one that says : "Be with, bless, be with, may we, let us, bless, be with. . . ."

As a leader of congregational prayer, you have a marvelous opportunity to expand the prayer vocabulary of the members of your community of faith. Most people, in fact, learn to pray by imitating what they hear their leaders of worship say in public prayers. If the prayers that you lead in the presence of others are vague and theologically weak, likely the same will become true in the personal prayer lives of your hearers. But if you set the example of approaching God boldly and specifically, your fellow worshipers will take courage and learn to pray in a similar manner, following the promises of God and the instruction Jesus gave to his followers.

Consider the following to be the first draft of a prayer. Where the verbs are less effective than they could be, substitute more vigorous verbs. In this exercise and most that follow, the lines are numbered in the left margin. This facilitates reference to them later. Please finish the editing task on this page before turning to the next page.

1   God of goodness and mercy: You are our help and strength in all the times of our lives.

2   We come to you with our concerns and petitions. Be with all who are distressed and

3   confused; give them your guidance. Let them know of your love. May we minister to

4   them. Especially we pray for the sick, that they may serve you in the fullness of body and

5   spirit. Be with all who suffer the ravages of storms, earthquakes, and other natural disasters.

6   Also be with those who endure famine and war. We pray for peace in the world. Let

7   anger and hostility give way to reconciliation. Bless your church with unity, so that

8   we may be an example of harmony and justice in a world torn by conflict. May your

9   people, both laity and clergy, find your will; and then let us have the courage to live out

10   your righteousness as a sign of your goodness. This we ask in the name and for the sake of

11   Jesus Christ, our Savior.

Do not proceed to the next page until you have completed your editing of the prayer above.

Suggested Revisions and Commentary

Read through the prayer as edited; then look carefully at the line-by-line comments that follow.

1   God of goodness and mercy: You are our help and strength in all the times of our lives.

              offer   Guide
2   We ~~come to~~ you ~~with~~ our concerns and petitions. ~~Be with~~ all who are distressed and

                                Assure them   By your power enable us to
3   confused~~; give them your guidance~~. ~~Let them know~~ of your love. ~~May we~~ minister to

                    Heal
4   them. ~~Especially we pray for~~ the sick, that they may serve you in the fullness of body and

                    Encourage and assist
5   spirit. ~~Be with~~ all who suffer the ravages of storms, earthquakes, and other natural disasters.

        Relieve the needs of   Establish   Cause
6   ~~Also be with~~ those who endure famine and war. ~~We pray for~~ peace in the world. ~~Let~~

                 to   Unite
7   anger and hostility ^ give way to reconciliation. ~~Bless~~ your church ~~with unity~~, so that

                                                Reveal your will to
8   we may be an example of harmony and justice in a world torn by conflict. ~~May~~ your

                                   Fill us with
9   people, both laity and clergy~~; find your will, and then let us have~~ the courage to live out

10   your righteousness as a sign of your goodness. This we ask in the name and for the sake of

11   Jesus Christ, our Savior.

Line 1. The opening form of the collect (address followed by attribution) can also serve at the beginning of a longer prayer. This line requires no alteration, but illustrates the principle just noted.

Line 2a. Although *come to* is acceptable, *offer* is stronger, reflecting the biblical conviction that prayer is a form of sacrifice presented to God. Recall the words of the psalmist:

Let my prayer be counted as incense before you,
     and the lifting up of my hands as an evening sacrifice. (Ps. 141:2)

Line 2b-3a. As previously noted, *be with* is at best the weakest of petitions. Since in line 3 we ask for guidance, the noun can readily be turned into a verb; thus the petition becomes: "Guide all who are distressed and confused."

Line 3b. *Let them know* is less direct and vigorous than *assure*.

Line 3c. *May we* leaves the realm of prayer and enters the realm of exhortation; that is to say, it is language directed at us, not at God. We are giving ourselves a pep talk rather than offering up a petition. Hence the change to "By your power enable us to." "Enable us to" would be sufficient. But the addition of "by your power" keeps focus on the fact that we need divine grace to assist us. *May we* deserves to be exiled from the vocabulary of Christian prayer. Note well, however, that the same does not apply to the phrase *that we may . . .* , which often begins the purpose portion of a collect or other prayer. (See lines 7-8 of this prayer, for example.) Tricky and subtle though it may seem, master the difference between *may we* (which is not a prayerful phrase) and *that we may* (which can be a very useful form in prayer).

Line 4. Again, "especially we pray for the sick" is not a petition, nor an act of praise or confession. It is simply a statement. Preceded by "may we" in the previous line, it continues to suggest that we are not at prayer at all, but simply engaged in a human conversation. *Heal* is a proper verb of petition. In later exercises we will come back to the phrase *we pray for* and its many weak-kneed cousins. Note that the petition is followed by a purpose ("that they may serve you in the fullness of body and spirit"). This illustrates the fact that the purpose section of the collect form can readily be transported into longer prayers. Inserting a purpose occasionally into a longer prayer breaks up what can become the somewhat monotonous quality of an extended series of brief petitions. If the prayer of Saint Basil quoted earlier in this section could be improved, it would be by making a couple of such insertions at key points.

Lines 5 and 6a. Again, *be with* is removed in favor of the far more vigorous *encourage* and *assist* in line 5, and in favor of *relieve the needs of* in line 6.

Line 6b. As in line 4, *we pray for* is a statement of fact, not a request.

Line 6c. *Let* is an anemic verb; the sentence can be interpreted as wishful thinking rather than petition. Substituting *cause* as the verb and inserting *to* before *give way* turns the statement into a petition.

Line 7. Use *bless* as a verb of petition only when nothing more direct appears to be available. But here the noun *unity* readily provides the more vigorous verb *unite*. (*Unify* is an equally good option.)

Line 8a. Note the acceptability of *we may* with the purpose that follows the petition. Review comments on lines 3 and 4 above concerning *may we* and *we may* to clarify and settle this matter in your mind.

Line 8b. There is no substantial difference between *may we* and *may your people*. Change the wish that the church may *find* God's will into an active request of God: *Reveal your will*.

Line 9. In prayer, *let us* is the twin sibling of *may we*. Both phrases address the congregation rather than God and therefore plead for human resolve rather than divine assistance. Hence the change.

Line 10. I have allowed "This we ask" to stand unaltered. However, it could be omitted, with the rest of the phrase appended to what precedes: "your goodness; in the name and for the sake of. . . . "

I strongly doubt that the editing you did will match the editing I have suggested. For one thing, yours likely will not be as thorough as mine. That is to be expected. After all, it has taken me four decades to develop whatever skills I have in this regard. Second, there is more than one way to accomplish change at a particular point in a prayer. Where I have changed *be with* to *guide*, you may have changed it to *direct* or *encourage*. The point is not that you should have done with this prayer exactly what I have done. But have you begun to recognize anemic verbs when you see them or to identify places where nouns could be turned into vigorous verbs? If so, you get an A for the day's work.

Interlude A

Patience and Persistence and Offerings to God

Today you may take a rest from the task of learning and simply allow me to give you some reassurance. You have now been introduced to the process of serious writing and editing in preparation for praying in public. At this juncture a very important distinction must be addressed concerning the difference between editing written prayers and praying extemporaneously. Often you will lead others in prayer without having written anything out, or even having given any thought to it. Particularly among the clergy, at least, this will happen rather frequently as people call upon you to pray aloud without asking you beforehand, or as an emerging situation requires prayer you have not foreseen. In such instances, likely you will frequently catch yourself using anemic verbs and phrases such as *may we* and *let us*. (Perhaps you have already caught yourself doing this!) Do not be alarmed, and try not to berate yourself when this occurs. There are at least three reasons why this will happen:

1. Until half a century ago, one translation of the Bible totally dominated Protestantism; active church members had segments of the translation memorized, or at least were thoroughly familiar with the usage of this Authorized (King James) Bible, even though it abounded in forms never used in conversation: *thee, thou,* and *thine, didst, wouldst, hast* and *hath, peradventure, trow,* and *adjure.* Public prayer clearly reflected that uniformity and familiarity. Now there are dozens of translations of the Bible in use, and to the declining extent that passages are memorized at all, these may well be taken from a wide variety of versions. Hence there is no longer a "language standard" against which to measure public prayer. Therefore we tend to learn to pray not by reading one particular translation of the Scriptures, but by listening to the great diversity of ways other people pray in public. This has led to a general decline of the biblical vocabulary of prayer, which in turn leads to the second difficulty.

2. Likely you have heard so many prayers filled with weak language that these seem quite natural and even beyond criticism because of the obvious sincerity of those who have offered the prayers. If you have led public prayers for a long time before reading this book, you undoubtedly have yourself used such words and phrases, just as I have in the past—and as I still do on occasion when praying extemporaneously. In other words, the use of weak prayer language has become a habit; like any other habit, it is difficult to break. Indeed, often it is not even recognized as being a matter in need of correction.

3. Particularly if you are called upon to pray in public without warning, you will necessarily insert some vagueness into the prayer. It takes more concentration to find the verb *enlighten* than to say *be with. Bless* will come to mind far more readily than *reveal* or *inspire.* Specificity of language comes less easily to all of us than does generality. (To see this phenomenon in a nonreligious setting, simply observe the difference in expression when the president of the United States is giving a prepared State of the Union Address and when the same president is holding an impromptu press conference after a crisis has suddenly emerged.)

As we will see in exercise 6, for the same reason you may fill up your impromptu prayer with phrases that do no real work, such as: "we pray that you would . . . " or "we come to you once again this evening asking that . . . ." In prayer, these are the equivalents of the *uhs* and *ers* with which we punctuate our answers to questions we were not expecting to come our way. Such words and syllables provide activity for our tongues while our brains are trying to think of what to say next. They are, therefore, quite natural. Still, that does not make them any less distracting or annoying to people who hear them. (God may not be bothered, but the same cannot always be said by those who are waiting to say the amen.) Hence the need to pray more fluently.

Because you are now becoming aware of the importance of selecting language carefully in prayer, when you use words that are weak or vague while praying "off the cuff," you may tend to berate yourself. Do not do so. You are simply experiencing the natural difference between editing on paper and praying *ex tempore*. So why continue to edit prayers—particularly if you are in a denominational or cultural tradition that frowns on "using prayers out of a book"?

I make you a promise: If you continue your written work, what you have learned by editing will creep into your unwritten prayers, even when you have not had opportunity to think about them in advance. The language of all of your prayers will become stronger and more direct (and thereby more biblical) because you have engaged in the hard task of careful language selection and revision.

But this will not happen within one week. Persistence and patience are required. The mastery of any new physical task—learning to type or play the piano for example—requires the establishing of new neural pathways in the brain. These are formed by repetitions that may seem utterly meaningless and boring during the learning process. (Recall "The quick brown fox jumps over the lazy dog" in typing class, or those awful Carl Czerny exercises your piano teacher foisted on you?) Similarly, new language pathways must be formed in the practice of prayer. Continue to edit on paper; and not only will you be more at ease when someone asks you on the spur of the moment to lead in prayer; your prayers on such occasions will gradually, perhaps almost imperceptibly, begin to reflect what you have done in writing, even though you may never take a piece of paper with you into the place of public prayer. (Whether you should take a written prayer with you is a matter to be considered in a later section of this manual). So keep to the task of working your way through this book and watch it happen!

But there is a deeper reason for seeking to improve public prayer. I said a moment ago that "God may not be bothered" by prayers that could be improved upon. I believe that. But at the same time God's image may be tarnished by careless speech. Recall what we have said about prayer being a form of offering to God, indeed a species of sacrifice. And the Bible is very emphatic that we must offer to God the very best sacrifice of which we are capable. It is to be a pure and unblemished lamb that is to be offered. (That is why Jesus is referred to as the true Lamb, for he alone is truly without spot or blemish.) In the Hebrew legislation concerning sacrifice, it is better to bring God a pair of perfect birds as an offering than a scruffy lamb. And a small portion of flour is preferred to two scraggly birds (see, for example, Leviticus 5:7, 11).

Nor can carelessness or casualness be excused by saying that "I am God's friend, and we are on the best of terms." That is indeed a reason why we may be utterly honest in prayer and why we may be bold in approaching God directly. But when we speak of serious matters to our closest earthly confidants, most likely we choose our words very carefully because we value communication with them and wish it to give rise to no misunderstanding or seeming disrespect. Surely it is no different in our friendship with God.

If the leader of prayer is a literate person with good facility in vocabulary and grammar, an ill-considered prayer offered by that person seems to suggest to the outsider: "The god of this person must not be worth very much, or this person would offer up something better. That is not the best of which this leader is capable." That is what I mean by suggesting that we may tarnish God's image by praying too casually or with too little preparation. If this happens, we unwittingly do a great disservice to evangelism. For we depict to the outsider a vision of God far inferior to the holy and exalted God of the Scriptures. At the same time, we may also offend the insider—the member of the community of faith who thinks (but almost never says to the leader), "I have something better to offer to God than you offered in my name. I cannot say a hearty amen because I earnestly desire to present to God something more than I just heard."

Recall that the first exercise in this book dealt with the grandeur of God. God is praised not only with words but with action. With regard to leading the prayers of the congregation, that action includes the careful preparation of disciplined thought and dignified speech. That is the deepest reason I can suggest to you for continuing the work you have begun here. The patience and persistence required to do this work are themselves crucial aspects of your offering of praise and thanksgiving to God.

Therefore it is my hope that you will come to see the work you do in this book not as a kind of schoolroom exercise to be done out of duty but as an act of worship to be offered up with joy. Equipping ourselves to pray more effectively is a form of honoring God, a way of declaring that God is worthy of our disciplined work. (And the term *worship* comes from the Anglo-Saxon word meaning "worth." To worship rightly is to proclaim that God is worthy, as the company of heaven does in the Revelation 4:11 and 5:2, 4, 9, and 12.)

Thereby claim as your own petition these words of the psalmist to God: "Let my prayer be counted as incense before you, and the lifting up of my hands [in prayer] as an evening sacrifice."

On Heaping Up Empty Phrases

Read Matthew 6:5-8.

In Matthew 6:7 Jesus precedes the giving of what we call the Lord's Prayer with this caution: "When you are praying, do not heap up empty phrases as the Gentiles do; for they think they will be heard because of their many words. Do not be like them." The prayer that Jesus then uses to teach his followers how to pray is the model of leanness and brevity. There is not a wasted word in it.

Consider how Jesus did **not** instruct us to pray: "Our Father in heaven, we want to come to you this evening hour asking you that your name might be hallowed. And Father, we also want to ask that your kingdom may come; and we pray earnestly to you that your will may be done, dear Father, on earth in the very same way that it is done in heaven. We pray that you would give us this day the bread, Father, which we need for our day's nourishment—just enough for today, Lord; that is all we ask; and we also want to pray that you would forgive us our many, many serious sins. . . . " You get the point. If ever you pray this way, you are by no means alone; nor am I trying to make you feel guilty about it. But we need to recognize that such inflated prayers tend to distract people who know well the biblical patterns of prayer and who take seriously Jesus' instruction in Matthew 6. Leaders of prayer are not to distract worshipers with such annoyances but to hold their attention, so that at the conclusion all can say with joy, "Amen!"

So why have we gotten into the habit of using such empty phrases? Likely there are two principal reasons: (1) We have not paid sufficient attention to the biblical patterns of prayer and do not even realize that we are heaping up empty phrases. We do well to spend more time with Scripture as our teacher, particularly the book of Psalms, which is the prayer book of the Bible. For biblical prayers are remarkably lacking in empty phrases such as "we come to you asking that" and "we pray that you would." (2) As noted in Interlude A, when we are praying extemporaneously, we use these empty phrases to "buy time" while we are trying to think of the appropriate petition to use. Note how these phrases tend to precede the verb of petition (and thus give us time to decide which verb we will use): "We pray that you would heal the sick."

These two reasons for heaping up empty phrases are understandable—even to some extent justifiable when we are called upon to pray without preparation. But lurking beyond these reasons may be yet a third, which has more serious implications regarding our faith. Many of the filler phrases act as distancing devices. To understand their function, consider this use of language in another set of circumstances. Suppose you are entering a worship space and want to sit in a certain seat. You need to sit next to the aisle because at a certain point you will have to leave your place to perform some function in the service. The row is not completely full, but a stranger is sitting at the aisle. Likely you will make a request something like this: "I wonder if it would be possible for you to move down one space?" or "Could I please ask you to move over one seat?" But if the person sitting in that seat were a close friend or family member, likely your request would be "Please move over" or even a somewhat abrupt "Move down." The phrases used with strangers make no literal sense. Of course it would "be possible" for the person to move. And not only "could" you ask the person to move, but you are actually asking. "Would it be possible . . . " and "Could I please ask . . . " are distancing phrases we use with persons we do not know well.

Prayer that is filled with overly polite or even somewhat apologetic phrases may suggest that we treat God as a stranger rather than a friend or parent. If "We want to come to you asking that you would" is not a device we use in extemporaneous prayer while we are trying to think of the petition we intend to state, then it may be a way of suggesting that we are less comfortable being direct with God than Jesus has taught us to be. That is a problem more related to faith development than to word choice; we need to consider well whether we experience God as one whom we love and trust, as a mere acquaintance, or even as a stranger to be approached with enormous caution.

Following the instruction of Jesus to avoid heaping up empty phrases, edit the following prayer. Also use the principles of editing you learned in earlier exercises. This prayer is suited to an occasion when you have been asked to pray at the anniversary of the establishment of a congregation.

1   God of Israel and of the church, we come to you knowing that throughout history you have

2   established communities of faith for the sake of your world. God, we want to thank you on this

3   occasion for the heritage and hope of our own congregation. We ask that you would keep before

4   us the example of the founders of this church, who struggled to bring us together as a sign of

5   your presence in this community. Let us be worthy of their example. May we take courage from

6   their perseverance and vision. We pray that we might carry into the future of this congregation

7   the spirit of faith and witness to God's love, which brought us to this celebration. We also want

8   to ask you to bless the other congregations in our community, that all of your people in this place

9   may present a united testimony to your love and power. We ask, O God, that you would make our

10   different congregations coworkers in your mission, not competitors. Finally, we come to you,

11   dear God, asking you to remember all churches across the earth. We pray that you would

12   bless them all and make them strong in their witness to Jesus Christ, through whom we pray.

Do not proceed to the next page until you have completed your editing of the above prayer.

Suggested Revisions and Commentary

1   God of Israel and of the church, ~~we come to you knowing that~~ throughout history you have

~~We~~
2   established communities of faith for the sake of your world. ~~God, we want to~~ thank you on this

Keep
3   occasion for the heritage and hope of our own congregation. ~~We ask that you would keep~~ before

4   us the example of the founders of this church, who struggled to bring us together as a sign of

Make us   Enable us to
5   your presence in this community. ~~Let us be~~ worthy of their example. ~~May we~~ take courage from

Motivate us to
6   their perseverance and vision. ~~We pray that we might~~ carry into the future of this congregation

your
7   the spirit of faith and witness to ~~God's~~ love, which brought us to this celebration. ~~We also want~~

Strengthen also
8   ~~to ask you to bless~~ the other congregations in our community, that all of your people in this place

Make
9   may present a united testimony to your love and power. ~~We ask, O God, that you would make~~ our

10   different congregations coworkers in your mission, not competitors. ~~Finally, we come to you,~~

Look graciously upon
11   ~~dear God, asking you to remember~~ all churches across the earth. ~~We pray that you would~~

Strengthen them
12   ~~bless them all and make them strong~~ in their witness to Jesus Christ, through whom we pray.

Lines 1-3. The reason for the revisions should be evident, with one elaboration. In line 2, the use of God's name is deleted, as also later in line 9. In a long prayer, it may be useful to address God more than once. Or sometimes a brief three-part prayer has its sections addressed to the persons of the Trinity, so that the prayer begins "O Gracious Father," but later is addressed to "O Jesus our Redeemer" and still later to "O Holy Spirit, ever present with us." But in a short prayer, periodically inserting the name of God may be distracting. Consider the awkwardness you feel if someone meets you on the street and says to you: "(*Name*), I am so glad to be able to see you today. I have been thinking about you, (*Name*), for several weeks now, (*Name*), and really intended to phone you. But, (*Name*), I just never got around to it; so it's good to run into you today, (*Name*)." Unless you are different from me, you begin to feel odd at being addressed by name so frequently.

Lines 5-7. Here we have stopped praying to God and moved into self-exhortation. This is revealed not only by the phrases "let us be" and "may we" but by reference to "God's love" in line 7. Beware of talking **about** God when you are supposed to be talking **to** God!

Lines 7-9. The reasons for the revision should be evident.

Lines 10-12. Beware when at prayer of saying *finally* or of doing any counting ("We ask first that . . . ." "Our second request is . . . "). This makes the prayer sound like a bad sermon. (Even inept preachers do not use the word *finally* unless they are within a few sentences of the end of the sermon!)

Now read aloud the original prayer (before your editing of it); then read aloud my revision of it. Finally read aloud your edited version. Can you tell the difference in the way the revised versions flow more smoothly once lazy language is removed? (I ask you to read these aloud because that is how they are used in worship, but also because some things are more noticeable to the ear than to the eye.)

Note also the general structure and content of this prayer. While it is directed at a local congregation's anniversary, it begins by setting this within the broad context of history: God has always been busy establishing communities of faith, and this God has done for the sake of the world, not just for the sake of individuals within one congregation. The prayer goes on to stress the role of the congregation as a sign of God's presence within the community. Then it asks God's equal blessing on other congregations in the community; and finally it extends its petitions to the whole church catholic (though it does not use such wording). There is embedded in this prayer a very deliberate theology of what it means to be the church.

All prayers contain theology because they are addressed to *theos* (the Greek word for God). When at prayer, you cannot avoid theology. The only question is "Will it be an accidental theology, not well thought out or poorly articulated; or will it be a deliberate theology, well stated?" Whichever it is, be certain that the congregation will learn from it.

At the opposite end of the spectrum from a sloppy theology, which teaches what we may not want to teach, is a heavy-handed theology in which the people who are trying to pray feel either bullied by the content or distracted by it. Often this occurs in the prayer that follows a sermon. The preacher, apparently unsure that the sermon itself has convinced the congregation, loads down the prayer by repeating within it the content of the sermon (as if God has not been listening and now needs to be informed of what it has just taken the preacher fifteen or twenty minutes to say).

We who lead in prayer must steer a careful course, falling neither into the trap of ill-considered or anemic theology, or into the morass of "laying it on so thick" that the worshipers think they have stumbled into a classroom lecture on abstract philosophical theology. But whatever course we take, we will express theology in some form every time we address God. Therefore, we do well to look carefully at the content of our prayer, as well as the form of praying.

Another Prayer Form: The Litany

Read Psalm 136.

At the close of the introduction, I asked you to begin each study session with prayer for yourself, asking God to make you a more capable leader of public prayer. If you have forgotten to include a personal prayer at the beginning of each exercise, please again take up that practice.

We look now at a form of prayer known as the litany. In popular use, *litany* seems to mean "a long list," as in "She poured out her litany of complaints about her supervisor at work." Usually, the tone of that usage is overwhelmingly negative. Almost never do we hear it said that "She recited a litany of joys and thanksgiving." But this casual use of *litany* is secondary and basically unrelated to the prayer form, except to the extent that in each instance a series of particulars is stated.

Originally *litany* meant a series of prayers offered by a leader in which the people could participate repeatedly by speaking or singing a fixed phrase or sequence of phrases. Both the ancient synagogue and church worked vigorously to make members of the congregation participants in prayer, not observers of it. There are to be no spectators at the worship of God. As noted in the opening section of this book, one way of achieving participation by all is the use of the unison "amen" at the close of a prayer. But in a long prayer, the people have to wait a significant time before they can speak their single word of approval. The litany form overcomes this disadvantage by breaking a long prayer into sections; at the end of each portion the congregation makes a suitable response. Psalm 136 is technically not a litany because it is a series of statements about God, not to God. But the repeated "for his steadfast love endures forever" may well have been a spoken or sung response that kept all present involved in the act of worship.

One of the most venerable forms of response is the Greek phrase, used in Christian worship since earliest times, *Kyrie eleison*, [KEE-rih-ay ee-LAY-ih-sawn]. The usual English translation—"Lord, have mercy upon us"—is not entirely a happy one, however, since it seems to suggest to us that we are in the midst of a prayer of confession and are seeking mercy from a God who is just, perhaps to the point of being harsh. The original connotation of the Greek was much more positive, meaning "Lord, show forth your goodness"; but for the most part we seem stuck with the negative translation. But there are many other suitable responses that can be used as alternatives to the Kyrie.

Originally worshipers held no books or service leaflets in their hands; and certainly they had neither an overhead projector nor a television monitor from which to read their words. If the prayer was sung, the leader (cantor) indicated by the tune when each petition was concluded; then the people sang their part. If the prayer was spoken, the leader used a fixed phrase at the end of each petition such as "Let us pray to the Lord." Then the people responded in unison: "Lord, have mercy," or "Lord, receive our prayer."

With the invention of the printing press and its subsequent descendants, litanies could become more complex within a literate congregation. Instead of having one fixed response, various responses could be said or sung at the close of the petitions.

Below is a litany for the fourth Sunday in Advent (the Sunday immediately before Christmas Day), which is based on the assigned scripture lessons for the day in Year C of the Revised Common Lectionary [Micah 5:2-5*a*; Luke 1:47-55; Hebrews 10:5-10; and Luke 1:39-45.] This litany is written in three portions; any one of the three can be used without the other two, or the three can be used in different parts of the service on the same day.

It is not necessary for the congregation to see a copy of this prayer, since each of their responses is the same and follows a common lead-in line. In order to join in the litany, the congregation needs to know its response and to understand that this response is preceded by the words, "You have done great things."

THANKSGIVING

We magnify and rejoice in you, God our mighty Savior.
For you have looked with favor on the lowly.
You scatter the proud and bring down the powerful,
   but you lift up the fallen and exalt the forgotten.
When any of your creatures are neglected, ill treated, or despised,
   you hasten to their defense and redeem them.
Truly, you have done great things,
    and holy is your name.

From the little tribe of Judah, from the obscurity of Bethlehem,
you have brought forth One
   who, by human reckoning, is David's descendant,
but who, by faith, is known to be your own Anointed.
This very One was given over to death and raised from the grave,
   that we who are dead in our sins might yet live by your mercy.
Truly, you have done great things,
    and holy is your name.

You have given us this season of Advent
   as a time appointed for nurturing hope amid the despair of life around us,
that we may trust in the promises made to our ancestors
   and to their descendants forever.
In these days of waiting and expectation,
you have called to our remembrance again and again
   the truth that you have done great things,
    and holy is your name.

INTERCESSION

Because of your goodness, O faithful God, we intercede for all who suffer,
especially those to whom the joy of this season seems a mockery,
   or at most a dream unrealized.
By the power of your Holy Spirit
   strengthen the weak of body and spirit,
   and console those who endure
     the devastations of inhumane action or of natural calamity.
This we ask, acknowledging that you have done great things,
    and holy is your name.

Particularly look graciously upon [*here may be inserted the specific needs within the congregation (particularly the ill and those who mourn or otherwise suffer greatly) and of the events and needs of the larger world that bear heavily on the hearts of the faithful*]. . . .
All these we remember knowing that you have done great things,
    and holy is your name.

To all who have hoped and waited long without reward,
give the joy bestowed on Elizabeth and Zechariah,
   when John was born to her who was considered barren.

For them, and in a myriad of other instances of grace toward your people,
    you have done great things,
        and holy is your name.

Direct the hearts and consciences of those who govern the peoples of the earth,
    that justice may find a home in every place,
    that greed and lust for power may be put aside
    for the sake of the common good and the welfare of every created thing.
Cause all to dwell in peace and security to the ends of the earth,
    according to the way of your holiness.
For you have done great things,
        and holy is your name.

PETITION

Reward us who wait upon you, O God,
    with surprises we cannot anticipate
As Mary was astounded by the announcement of Gabriel,
    so also amaze us with promises beyond our comprehension,
    even with responsibilities we fear to accept.
To us, speak the word
    that the power of the Holy Spirit will come upon us
    and the power of the Most High overshadow us,
        that we may fulfill all you have assigned to us.
For you have done great things,
        and holy is your name.

In these final hours of waiting to celebrate the coming of our Lord,
    prepare us to plumb the depths of the mystery of incarnation
        and to ponder the mystery of your final judgment and reign.
Enable us to bear the fruits of repentance,
    lest the outward customs of Christmas be observed by us
        without the inward reality of faith being enacted in life each day.
Inhabit us continually with your Living Word,
    as for centuries you have filled your people with transforming love.
You have done great things,
        and holy is your name.

To us and to your Church spread across the whole earth,
to faithful Christians of every race and station in life,
    give a faithful observance of the Nativity.
To all bring again that good news of great joy;
so satisfy the cravings of the human heart that,
    having seen the great thing come to pass,
        your people may glorify and praise you for all we have seen and heard,
            even as it has been told to us by the chorus of angelic voices.
Gracious are you, O God, and righteous for ever and ever.
And once again we proclaim with joy that you have done great things,
        and holy is your name.

To you be all honor and power and thanksgiving and praise, through Jesus Christ our Savior.
    Amen.

Here is another litany, intended for January 6, or the Sunday on which the Epiphany is observed. The prayer is based on the story of the coming of the Magi and the meaning of their symbolic gifts. In this case, the congregation has various responses throughout the prayer. This assumes a literate congregation and a text all can see.

The Lord be with you.
    And also with you.
Let us pray.

Holy Ruler of the universe,
    Eternal Word through whom all things were made:
By the gold of your majesty, enrich the poor of the earth
    —the destitute and hungry, the homeless and the helpless—
    and ennoble all whose lives have been trampled
        by deliberate oppression or cruel circumstance.
Confound the Herods of our age
    whenever they set out to destroy the children in our midst,
    and whenever they oppose
        that which is sent from heaven to save the earth.
But multiply the works of all who seek peace and do what is right.
Creator of all worlds,
    receive our prayer and put within us glad and generous hearts.

Emmanuel,
    God's Messiah sent to live among us:
Raise up sages who journey from afar,
    to inquire into your ways,
    and to proclaim to all your worthiness.
By the frankincense of your divinity, transform all mortal flesh,
    that we may receive your nature into us,
        even as you have taken our nature upon yourself.
Quietly infuse our disheveled world with graciousness:
As once you came silently and incognito into the chaos
        of an over-crowded census town,
    so again and again come among us and reside with us,
        ordering our lives according to the strange ways of your righteousness.
Holy Presence in our midst,
    receive our prayer and conform us to your image.

Suffering Servant,
    and Shepherd of your people:
By the myrrh of your terrible torture,
        of your humiliating, unwarranted execution,
        and of your ignoble burial in a borrowed crypt:
Bring relief to all who endure the indignities and agonies of life;
    sustain and vindicate those who are made to suffer unjustly;
        and to the dying and their mourners
            give the consolation of your presence,
            that Rachel need weep no longer for her lost children.
Out of your exile in Egypt bring forth goodness,
    and set at liberty all captives.
Savior of the world,
    receive our prayer and rescue us,
    that we may freely serve you and all that you have made. Amen. [8]

These two litanies are relatively complex in form; they are not the type of prayer you are editing or writing at this stage. Their grammatical construction is sufficiently complex that the leader of these litanies needs to rehearse them carefully in order to read them well. (And a poorly read litany unjustly gives written prayers a bad name.) But these two prayers do illustrate the way in which litanies based on specific biblical passages can be written for use on particular occasions.

Now it is time for you to try your hand at writing a litany—simpler in design than those above, but based on something that will provide unity and direction. So rather arbitrarily I ask you to write a litany based on the Beatitudes of Matthew 5:3-12. Since *beatitude* means "blessedness," or "happiness," each response by the congregation will be: *O Lord, grant us this blessing.*

I suggest below how the first Beatitude might be embodied in prayer and then ask you to do the rest. Although each Beatitude is printed here, these would not necessarily be read as a part of the prayer. If they are used as part of the litany, it may be well to have them read by a person other than the one who states the petitions. Alternatively, Matthew 5:3-12 as a whole could be read first and then the petitions and response be used, omitting the separated Beatitudes as they appear below.

Blessed are the poor in spirit, for theirs is the kingdom of heaven.
Enable us, gracious God, in the poverty of our spirits, to love and be received into
your heavenly kingdom.
O Lord, grant us this blessing.

Blessed are those who mourn, for they will be comforted.

_____

_____

_____

O Lord, grant us this blessing.

Blessed are the meek, for they will inherit the earth.

_____

_____

O Lord, grant us this blessing.

Blessed are those who hunger and thirst for righteousness, for they will be filled.

_____

_____

O Lord, grant us this blessing.

Blessed are the merciful, for they will receive mercy.

_____

_____

O Lord, grant us this blessing.

Blessed are the pure in heart, for they will see God.

_____

_____

_____

O Lord, grant us this blessing.

Blessed are the peacemakers, for they will be called children of God.

_____

_____

_____

O Lord, grant us this blessing.

Blessed are those who are persecuted for righteousness' sake, for theirs is the kingdom of heaven.

_____

_____

_____

O Lord, grant us this blessing. Amen.

When you have finished:
1. Look over your work for faithfulness to the Beatitudes. Is each petition intimately related to that Beatitude, and that one alone?
2. Check your work for grammatical consistency. Does each petition largely follow the form of the previous ones? (A litany requires a variety of words within a fairly fixed form.)
3. Recall the principles of editing learned in previous exercises, and check your work as to the strength of its verbs and the absence of empty words.
4. Try reading the entire litany aloud to see whether it sounds flowing and graceful or disjointed and awkward.
5. Revise as necessary.

Exercise 8

Achieving Variety and Breadth

Read Psalm 65.

As indicated in exercise 6, inescapably prayers contain theology; and those who hear them will, for good or ill, learn theology from them. Therefore if you lead prayers on a regular basis, it is useful to determine whether these are very constricted in expression and content or whether they have a variety and breadth to them. Not only will constricted prayers put forth a narrow band of theology, but they may become so predictable as to be boring. Congregations do not take well to prayer leaders whose language becomes so unimaginative that the listener can finish the leader's sentence just by hearing the opening words.

I am presenting here ways in which you can check on variety and breath by analyzing prayer manuscripts you have written. If you always pray without a manuscript (or without notes derived from one), it is advisable to make audio recordings of your prayers with some regularity. From the audiotape, transcribe a typed copy so that you can look at the page after the fact in the same way you would look at the page of a manuscript written beforehand. This requires work, but it helps to prevent a deadly predictability.

To illustrate this method of analysis, I will give you another litany, briefer and of a different design from those in exercise 7. This litany is not based on any set of lectionary readings or other biblical passage. It is "a general litany," covering a range of causes; it could be used at a Sunday service to sum up concerns expressed by members of the congregation.

Almighty and most gracious God:
Look with compassion upon your creation.
By your power, transform all that falls short of your design for us,
    and minister to all who are in need.
Lord in your mercy:
Receive our prayer.

Especially we remember those known to us
    who are sick or who mourn.
[*Here specific names may be inserted.*]
Heal their bodies and comfort their spirits with your love.
Lord in your mercy:
Receive our prayer.

Restore hope and dignity to any
    who suffer under the ravages of war,
    who flee their lands as refugees,
    who are hungry or left homeless
        by earthquake, storm, and other disaster.
Lord in your mercy:
Receive our prayer.

Give wisdom and a passion for justice to all who govern us,
    particularly the president of the United States,

the members of the Congress,
   and the Supreme Court,
that they may earnestly and with honesty pursue the welfare of all people.
Lord in your mercy:
Receive our prayer.

Strengthen all in every nation
   who strive for peace and work for righteousness.
Encourage them with your word of reconciliation,
and grant them wisdom and patience in all of their endeavors.
Lord in your mercy:
Receive our prayer.

Increase the faithfulness and obedience of your whole church
   in witness and service,
    that thereby the world may be drawn to understand more fully
     your will and your ways.
Lord in your mercy:
Receive our prayer.

Graciously accept these and all of our prayers,
and according to your wisdom do what is best for us;
through Jesus Christ our Savior. ***Amen.***

One way to evaluate the draft of a prayer such as this general litany is to mark the verbs of petitions in one color of ink or highlighting pen, the persons and causes prayed for in a second color, and the attributes of God stated or implied in a third color. Then arrange these categories in columns, as follows.

Verbs of Petition	Persons/Causes	Divine Attributes
look	creation	almighty
transform	all that falls short	gracious
minister	those in any need	compassionate
heal	the sick	powerful
comfort	those who mourn	loving
restore	those who suffer war	reconciling
give	refugees	wise
strengthen	the hungry	
encourage	the homeless	
grant	U.S. president	
increase	Congress	
accept	Supreme Court	
do	workers for peace	
	church catholic	

Read down each list (not across the page) to determine whether a prayer includes a goodly range of concerns and theological breadth. Not everything can be put in a brief prayer on the same Sunday. Therefore if you lead in prayer regularly, it may be useful to compare such lists over a period of months to determine what has not been held before God in prayer recently. (There is a great irony in the fact that some persons and groups reject a prayer book or any form of prepared prayers because they fear these will make prayer routine and shallow. But when self-discipline is not exercised, "extempore" prayers led by the same person week after week can become even more predictable and limited in scope than any good collection of printed prayers. Therefore test yourself in a disciplined way.)

Such a listing as shown above also can reveal what is being overlooked. For example, my personal experience within the United States is that while the president is mentioned frequently in prayer, Congress (implying both Senate and House) is the object of prayer less often, and the Supreme Court is mentioned rarely, if at all. The kind of listing done above enables you to see such inconsistencies, if they exist.

On the occasion for which the above litany was written, I chose to pray for the church in general terms. At other times I would pray specifically for my own (or another) denomination and its particular leaders. And since most denominations have various geographical levels of organization (local, regional, national, international), a rotation of petitions can enable the church to pray for the full range of its leadership over time. Again, comparing lists over time will reveal whether you are achieving a good balance of prayer for the church at various levels or whether only a few aspects of the life of the church are being expressed in your prayers.

Note that the litany contains two purpose clauses, of the kind we first identified in the collect form. In the petition for governmental leaders, the stated purpose is "that they may earnestly and with honesty pursue the welfare of all people." In the petition for the work of the church the purpose is "that thereby the world may be drawn to understand more fully your will and your ways." Having purposes stated for some (but not all) petitions is another way of lending variety to a prayer.

Now try your own hand at writing a litany such as the one just considered; follow these specifications:

1. While there is no magic number of petitions to be included, for this exercise write six to eight petitions. (Arabic numbers below are for your guidance only, and would not appear in a published prayer.)
2. Make your prayer useful for a particular occasion (such as next Sunday or Easter Day).
3. Decide on a common ending for each petition and a common corporate response to each petition, so that the congregation does not need to look at the text in order to know when to make the unison response.

The common ending to each petition is: _____

The common response to each petition is: _____

Petition 1 _____
_____
_____
_____

Petition 2 _____
_____
_____
_____

Petition 3 _____
_____
_____
_____

Petition 4 _____
_____
_____

Petition 5 _____

_____

_____

_____

Petition 6 _____

_____

_____

_____

Petition 7 _____

_____

_____

_____

Petition 8 _____

_____

_____

_____

When the first draft of the prayer is completed:

1. Look over it and make initial editorial changes, as in previous exercises.
2. Make lists of verbs of petition, persons/causes, and divine attributes. Note duplications and omissions.

Verbs of Petition	Persons/Causes	Divine Attributes

3. For the sake of variety, did you include any purpose clauses with your petitions? How many?
4. Again edit your text.
5. Read the prayer aloud to see if it is felicitous to the tongue and ear.
6. If necessary, make a final revision.

Interlude B

To Write or Not to Write: Is *That* the Question?

Thus far we have been working with texts, yet have alluded to a crucial question, which I now address head-on: "Should those who are asked to lead in prayer write out what they intend to say?"

Convincing arguments can be raised on both sides. Writing is an important discipline that can help us to organize our thoughts and pare our expression to a proper length. But some people seem not to be able to deal with a written prayer in a way that sounds sincere and alive. (It appears to matter little whether the prayer is of their own authorship or taken from a book.) Hence it is easy to assume that a written prayer is necessarily a "read prayer" in the worst sense of that term. Prayers, this line of thinking concludes, should never be written out because "a read prayer is a dead prayer."

But note that while the fault can lie in the composition (if its construction is clumsy and its vocabulary stilted), more often the difficulty is not in the writing but in the inept use of what has been written. The complaint is that the prayer sounds "read," not "prayed." That is, there is a noticeable dependence upon a document, which leads to problems such as a flatness of pitch, or a pattern of inflection that is predictable, or the kind of stammering over words that occurs more in reading than in conversation.

For people who are inexperienced at prayer leadership, the issue is not "to write or not to write" but "to read or not to read." By all means do the necessary writing. But then, perhaps, leave the manuscript on your desk or in your pocket, or reduce it to notes if you do not have the ability to read documents aloud with interest and ease. The act of writing will serve to clarify and organize your content in a way that simply thinking about what you are going to say may not do. Indeed, that is why many find writing to be so difficult; it forces us to do the hard work of planning that otherwise we are apt to kid ourselves into thinking we have done, even if we have not.

Note well that this is a recommendation for those who are inexperienced at public prayer. Experience builds both skill and confidence; at a later stage you may or may not need the discipline of writing a prayer out, word for word. But at the beginning most people will benefit greatly from putting ink to paper. The art of good writing is the act of thorough editing. As you have already discovered from the exercises, much that is written as a preliminary draft can be deleted, replaced, or refined for the sake of clarity and conciseness.

Writing also has the potential of allowing you to catch ahead of time unintended humor or double meaning—though on this point, it is well to show your proposed prayer to someone else, since you may be unable to catch such things in your own writing. In order to protect the guilty, I will omit to document the sources of two prayers I am about to cite. But both were offered by persons who had risen to the eminence of bishop, one a United Methodist, and the other an Episcopalian; but I will not even reveal which bishop uttered which hilarious sentence. (I provide this much identification simply to demonstrate that unintended humor or double meaning resulting from lack of editing can afflict even the most experienced of prayer leaders.)

One prayer was given on the occasion of the dedication of a health-care center in a retirement community. Imagine the scene. The people gathered are for the most part very elderly, and the health-care center is largely for the terminally ill. Said the bishop: "As we come here today, we face grave tasks. . . ." Not exactly the right choice of words, and some who heard them were too amused to continue in an attitude of prayer. Still more distracted were those who heard the other bishop. Offering a prayer at the groundbreaking for a new church building, this bishop implored the Lord to "Bless this erection." I am not making these examples up; I could not have thought of anything that funny on my own! These two instances in the ministries of very prominent clerics should be ample warning to any (and particularly to the inexperienced) who want to skip writing and carefully editing in their preparation for public prayer.

Here is another advantage to preparing a manuscript. If the time allotted for prayer is crucial, a manuscript provides some gauge. How long it will take you to pray one page depends on how rapidly you speak, how wide the margins and spaces between the lines are, and what size print is used. Each person will have to determine by experience how long delivery takes per page. Once this is determined, future attempts to stay within a prescribed time range can be successful. Gauging time is a way of fulfilling the expectation of those who invite you to pray; it is rude to pray for ten minutes if you were asked to confine the prayer to two minutes. The ability to conform to time constraints based on a prepared text will also reduce the anxiety that arises from worrying whether a prayer is too long, too short, or about right.

Now to amplify the earlier suggestion concerning alternatives if you cannot master the use of a manuscript during the service of worship. If you decide to use nothing written at all while leading in prayer, at least carry with you what you have prepared in case you draw a complete blank when stepping to the lectern or when kneeling at the prayer desk. Simply having your manuscript handy can be a helpful reassurance against the fear of panic. Even reading a manuscript rather poorly is better than succumbing to a state of silence or of being able to utter nothing other than "errrr" and "uhhhh." And memory lapses do occur, even to the most experienced of those who pray in public.

There are, however, alternatives to the all-or-nothing approach to the manuscript. Having written the prayer out to your satisfaction, you can then reduce it to something less than a full manuscript. Suppose your manuscript for a prayer of intercession includes this:

Gracious God, your love and mercy surround us in every task we face. We have the testimony of faithful people across the centuries to your dependable goodness. Therefore, we bring you both praise and petition. Look with mercy upon all who suffer the ravages of war, the agony of famine, and the destruction of natural disasters. Comfort those who mourn, and give the assurance of your faithful presence to those for whom death is near. Draw close to the sick with healing power, and give wisdom and patience to all who minister to them.

Reduced to ample notes (rather than a word for word text), what you take with you may look like this:

Love, mercy surround us.
Testimony of faithful people
    to dependable goodness.
Bring praise and petition.
Look upon all who suffer:
    ravages of war,
    agony of famine,
    destruction of disaster.
Comfort—mourners.
Reassure—dying.
Draw close—sick.
Give those who minister
    wisdom, patience...

Such notes will not enable you to give the prayer you wrote word for word; but they will assure that the gist of the manuscript is there. Supplying the missing words "on your own" so to speak, may make the prayer sound authentic rather than "read." (Notice that I have not included the address to God in the notes; almost certainly you can provide an address *ex tempore*. But if not including it causes you anxiety, by all means add the address to your notes.)

Some who are to lead in prayer and have prepared the above text may want to reduce the manuscript even further, listing the concerns only in the barest form:

Praise of God.
Testimony of others.

Petitions:
    War, famine, disaster;
    mourners, dying;
    sick and those who help.

This form enables you to reconstruct the prayer more fully "on the spot," yet avoids the panic that can set in if you have no reminder at all of what you planned. But these sparse notes do not include verbs of petition and will be of limited use to anyone who has difficulty selecting vigorous verbs.

There is no single way of adapting the prepared manuscript that will suit everyone who prefers not to read from it directly. By a process of experimentation you can arrive at your own best use of what you have prepared in advance. You may discover that what you use will vary from occasion to occasion, depending upon differences in the setting within which you work and upon your growing confidence. For example, leading in prayer at an informal service on Wednesday evening is far less likely to produce anxiety within you than praying at the funeral where the family of the deceased is emotionally over-wrought and many prominent citizens are in attendance. Based on that kind of difference in setting, you may decide to prepare your prayer notes in two quite different ways.

In some cases you may be asked to—or choose to—use prayers others have written. Then you will not deviate from their language and will need to have the word-for-word text in front of you, even if you never take to the place of praying a word-for-word version of what you yourself have written. But you may well want to alter the form in which the words of the author appear on the page. Perhaps the size of print is not large enough in the book where the prayer appears; or you may want to put a margin-to-margin text into the form of sense lines for ease of reading. (In exercise 9, we will consider more fully the use of sense lines.) You may decide to underline or highlight words to which you wish to give particular stress by the use of your voice. You may also want to mark places at which you intend to pause for the sake of emphasis. However you proceed, careful preparation with a view to complete familiarity with the text is the key. Not only will you wish to pronounce all words correctly; you will also want to convey clearly the meaning of what another person has written in a way that edifies all who are to join in the amen.

When interpreting a prayer written by someone else, take great care in trying to determine where the emphasis properly belongs. A helpful exercise in this regard is to ask what an emphasized word implies by way of contrast. Saying "*Give* me that book" suggests that I am not willing to buy it. "Give *me* that book" implies "Do not keep it yourself. I want it." Or it may mean "Give it to me, not to the person standing next to me." "Give me *that* book" indicates I want the volume you have in your hand, not any of several dozen books on a nearby shelf. And if I say "Give me that *book*," I may be suggesting that you can keep the magazine you also have in your hand. Proper vocal emphasis is crucial to good communication, and usually such emphasis implies some kind of contrast.

Sometimes the author of the prayer will have set up the contrasts for us very clearly. Here is how I would interpret part of the familiar prayer attributed to Saint Francis of Assisi:

Grant that I may not so much seek
    to be *consoled*, as to *console*;
    to be *understood*, as to *understand*,
    to be *loved*, as to *love*;
for it is in *giving* that we *receive*,
it is in *pardoning* that we are *pardoned*,
and it is in *dying* that we are *born* to eternal *life*. [9]

The contrasts were set up by the author. Only someone who pays no attention to meaning would read it in this way:

Grant that I may not so much seek
to be consoled, as *to* console;
to be understood, as *to* understand,
to be loved, as *to* love;

for it *is* in giving that *we* receive,
it *is* in pardoning that *we* are pardoned,
and it *is* in dying that *we* are born to eternal life.

Here is a prayer written by Erasmus (1469–1536) when he was ill. Consider what words you might emphasize in reading it aloud, and how you might write it out for such use:

Lord Jesus Christ, you are the only source of health for the living, and you promise eternal life to the dying. I entrust myself to your holy will. If you wish me to stay longer in this world, I pray that you will heal me of all my present sickness. If you wish me to leave this world, I readily lay aside this mortal body, in the sure hope of an immortal body which shall enjoy everlasting health. I ask only that you relieve me of pain, that whether I live or die, I may rest peaceful and contented.[10]

I would arrange it for my own oral use as follows:

Lord Jesus Christ,
you are the *only* source
    of *health* for the *living*,
and you promise
    life to the *dying*.
I entrust myself
    to your *holy will*.
If you wish me to *stay* longer in *this* world,
    I pray that you will *heal* me
        of all my *present sickness*.
If you wish me to *leave* this world,
    I readily lay aside this *mortal* body
        in the sure hope of an *immortal* body
            which shall enjoy *everlasting* health.
I ask only that you relieve me of *pain*,
    that whether I *live* or *die*,
    I may rest *peaceful* and *contented*.

This is not the only possible interpretation of the text, but it does highlight the contrasts, such as stay/ leave, mortal/immortal and live/die. Certainly it is not the first person pronouns (I/myself/me) that call for emphatic expression. At points, the second person pronouns might be emphasized, so that the second line could be read: "*You* are the only source," suggesting that it is vain to trust in anyone other than God. There is no single correct interpretation. Nor is there only one way of arranging the words on a page.

Here are some decisions crucial to the good oral interpretation whether the prayer is your own or someone else's:
    1. Have clearly in mind where you want to place vocal emphasis.
    2. Decide how you will achieve vocal emphasis in each instance:
        by saying the words with more force,
        by raising or lowering the pitch of the voice,
        by extending or shortening the length of the vowels,
        by the use of a well-placed pause,
        by some other means,
        or by some combination of these.
    3. Having decided all of this, prepare the kind of manuscript or notes you find most useful.

Whether you use a prayer written by someone else or one you have composed yourself, whether you use your own manuscript word-for-word or reduce it to something less extensive, do the careful preparation necessary to be a good leader in public prayer. Challenge the notion that the Holy Spirit can work more effectively with someone who is unprepared than with someone who has given thought and care in advance to the task of praying.

If you distrust my counsel and seek a second opinion, here is one from Fred Craddock. Many people, he notes, reject the idea of preparation for public prayer. They believe "you catch prayer. It's natural, they say. You just pray. 'We just thank you for this . . . we just pray for that.' I once thought that myself," confesses Craddock, who goes on to tell of his encounter with a seminary professor who gave the class an assignment to write a prayer. "*Write* prayers?" thought young Craddock. "When you come out of the back country of Tennessee, as I did, you don't write prayers. A written prayer is not from the heart. A written prayer is not sincere."

So seminarian Craddock knocked on the door of his professor's office to make his protest. To the student's objection that prayers should be spontaneous, Dr. Osborn responded: "Can't the Holy Spirit help you prepare the prayer? Can't the Holy Spirit be with you in the study?" Osborn continued on and on in this vein, according to Craddock, until "by the end of our conversation I felt like two cents waiting for change. I now believe that preparation for prayer does not interfere with the Spirit. I believe that spontaneity interferes with the Spirit. Spontaneously, I just think, and feel, and say the things I think and feel. By contrast, the reign of God demands that I do things that I do not want to do, and say things I do not want to say, and go places I do not want to go. Spontaneity gives me a way to hide from that."[11]

Spontaneity interferes with the Sprit and gives us a way to hide from the demands of God? Indeed so! And disciplined preparation is the Spirit's gift.

One final word about the benefits of writing out prayers in certain circumstances. If the service of worship is being interpreted in sign language, those who do the signing prefer to have in advance as many of the texts used in the service as possible (scripture readings, hymn stanzas, sermon manuscript, creed, the words of solos or anthems, and so on). If you have written out the full prayer, signers will appreciate receiving your manuscript before the service begins. This greatly facilitates their work and enables persons who depend on sign language to participate more fully in the service.

Exercise 9

Corporate Prayers of Confession

Read Psalm 139.

Thus far we have dealt with prayers whose content consists largely of attributions about God and petitions to God, together with purposes stated for some of the petitions. We turn now to another central form of Christian public prayer—the corporate confession.

The prayer of confession itself is surrounded by related acts. It is usually preceded by a call or invitation to confession. In the past, some of these were rather long and complex, but it is sufficient to say, "Together let us make our confession to God," or even simply, "Let us confess our sin." After the prayer there may be a period of silence, either for reflection on what has just been said or as an opportunity for individuals silently to make personal confessions of particular sins.

Then there is a declaration of pardon or assuring words. Often these are taken from scripture, such as 1 John 1:9, "If we confess our sins, he who is faithful and just will forgive us our sins and cleanse us from all unrighteousness." There may then be a congregational response, such as a hearty "Thanks be to God." In some denominations instead of, or in addition to, a scripture sentence, there may be a prescribed authoritative clerical statement such as: "By the authority given to me at my ordination, I declare unto you a full and complete absolution of all of your sins." But all of these matters are usually established by denominational liturgies or strong local custom. What concerns us here is the prayer of confession itself.

The corporate prayer of the congregation has traditionally been called a "general confession," and that title deserves to be taken seriously. *General* implies a contrast to *specific*, even as *corporate* implies a contrast to *individual*. Herein lies a crucial matter: Some things that individuals may quite appropriately confess to God in private are not the proper subjects of public prayer. Therefore those who write prayers of confession need to note carefully what is and what is not fitting, lest the author of the prayer impose her or his own personal sins on a congregation not guilty of the same offenses.

I frequently arrive early enough for worship to read over the bulletin before the service starts. On one such occasion, in the prayer of confession I noticed a statement that astonished me. The entire congregation was going to be asked to say, "I hate my body. I wish I had a different one." While I may wish I had more hair, and would prefer not to have to spend so much time in the dentist's chair, my body has been unusually and consistently healthy for more than sixty years. I do not hate my body. I would not trade it for another, and I cannot in good conscience offer to God an insincere prayer simply because it is put into print and handed to me by an usher. So when we came to those words in the prayer, I fell silent.

The three occasions of the word *I* in the offending prayer should have been a warning sign to whoever wrote that prayer that it was not appropriate for public worship. General prayers of confession are universally expressed in the plural: *we, us, our, ours,* not *I, me, my, mine*." But the situation would have been little better had the prayer read, "We hate our bodies; we wish we had different ones." For above all, prayer needs to be honest. In private, an individual may appropriately confess "I covet my neighbor's new car." In public we should not be asked to say: "We covet the new cars owned by our neighbors," for something that specific applies only to a few of those present. Therefore public confession is general: "We covet what does not belong to us."

Note the generality of the centuries-old confession that has passed down through English-speaking Protestantism (given below in contemporary wording rather than the traditional "thee" and "thou" vocabulary). As a way of illustrating

59

how immersed some of the old prayers are in the language of Scripture, the biblical allusions are also supplied. (The language used is usually either that of the 1611 Authorized Version translated in the time of King James or one of its predecessors. Because these translations are so rarely consulted these days, and because Bible reading in general has so declined, we are barely able any longer to recognize these allusions when we hear them. How unfortunate for us!)

Almighty and most merciful God,
we have erred and strayed from your ways
   like lost sheep.   (Isaiah 53:6; Psalm 119:176; 1 Peter 2:25)
We have followed too much
   the devices and desires of our own hearts.   (Proverbs 19:21; Jeremiah 18:12)
We have offended against your holy laws.   (2 Chronicles 28:13)
We have left undone those things
   which we ought to have done;
and we have done those things
   which we ought not to have done.   (Matthew 23:23)
And there is no health in us.   (Psalm 38:3)
O Lord, have mercy upon us, miserable offenders.   (Psalm 51:1; Luke 18:13)
Spare those who confess their faults.   (Nehemiah 13:22)
Restore those who are penitent,   (Psalm 51:12)
according to your promises declared   (Romans 15:8)
   unto us in Christ Jesus our Lord.
And grant, O most merciful Father,
   for his sake,   (1 John 2:12)
that we may hereafter live a godly, righteous,
   and sober life,   (Titus 2:12)
to the glory of your holy name. Amen.   (John 14:13)

The general character of the language allows each person who prays to supply mentally specific things done or left undone. In its outline, however, this formulation reveals what a comprehensive prayer of confession might contain:

Address to God, as One from whom mercy can be expected.
Confession of wrongful acts and/or good acts not done.
Request for pardon.
Intention of amendment of life.
Closing.

The form of this prayer is not far from that of a collect, though it is significantly longer. Between the address and the petition, the confession is inserted. What is crucial is the purpose stated: "that we may hereafter live a godly, righteous, and sober life." Too many prayers of confession neglect this, and thus may seem to suggest that we intend to go right on sinning. As a matter of fact, we *will* continue to be sinners; but if we *intend* so to be, that is a significantly different matter. However far short we may fall of them, intentions are important. Seeking divine help in order to move forward toward keeping those intentions is crucial to a Christian act of confession. Repentance means making a U-turn. If we are content to keep going in the same direction, we mock God's gracious desire to forgive and ignore God's great power to transform.

These are matters of content. But something must also be said about the literary form of unison prayers. If such prayers are to be understood by a congregation (not merely read in mechanical fashion), the vocabulary and grammatical structure need to be simple. When words are unfamiliar or sentences are long and complex, the people get bogged down in the mechanics of reading and may miss the meaning of what they are saying. This is most especially true if a prayer is new to them. Prayers that are used repeatedly get bad press. In truth, when a prayer is familiar (as distinct from overly familiar to the point of being worn out), we may be free enough from having to worry about where to pause and which words to emphasize to be able to grasp the deep meaning of what we are saying to God. We need to challenge the prevailing notion that all good contemporary prayers should be disposable—used only once or twice, then thrown out. Still, every prayer is new to a congregation at some point, and we need to take care to keep fresh language simple enough to be read in unison without difficulty.

Now try your hand at editing the following text.

1   God of judgement and compassion, we ask that you would look upon us with mercy. We know

2   that you have called us to do your will, but we have ignored your will and your ways to the point that

3   we are like rebellious children who, having heard the parental call, run in the opposite direction

4   to hide, rather than do what is being asked of them. We have been selfish rather than gracious;

5   and as a result of this we have failed to set before the world an example of your goodness, which

6   you have called us to do. We have not shown sufficient concern for our family and friends and

7   have neglected the disciplines of daily prayer and Bible reading. We have not given the tithes

8   due to you, Holy God. Have mercy upon us, O Lord, for we lack the quality of magnanimity.

9   We pray for those whom we have offended or neglected. Grant them the capacity to forgive us

10   for whatever we have done or failed to do. Improve their lives according to your wisdom.

11   Bestow upon them and upon us your favor and mercy, even as you offer your divine goodness

12   to the whole world, which you have redeemed through the grace of Christ our Savior.

Do not proceed to the next page until you have completed your editing of the above prayer.

Suggested Revisions and Commentary

judgment

1 God of ~~judgement~~ and compassion, ~~we ask that you would~~ look upon us with mercy. ~~We know~~

You

2 ~~that you~~ have called us to do your will, but we have ignored your ~~will and~~ ways ~~to the point that~~

We   children. We have heard your call; but we have

3 ~~we~~ are like rebellious ~~children who, having heard the parental call,~~ run in the opposite direction

We hide from you, rather than doing what you ask.   gracious.

4 ~~to hide, rather than do what is being asked of them.~~ We have been selfish rather than ~~gracious,~~

We

5 ~~and as a result of this we~~ have failed to set before the world an example of your goodness, which

6 you have called us to do. ~~We have not shown sufficient concern for our family and friends, and~~

7 ~~have neglected the disciplines of daily prayer and Bible reading. We have not given the tithes~~

too often we fail to be generous.

8 ~~due to you, Holy God.~~ Have mercy upon us, O Lord, for ~~we lack the quality of magnanimity.~~

[See in the commentary the reconstruction of the prayer from this point forward.]

9 ~~We pray for those whom we have offended or neglected. Grant them the capacity to forgive us~~

10 ~~for whatever we have done or failed to do. Improve their lives according to your wisdom.~~

11 ~~Bestow upon them and upon us your favor and mercy, even as you offer your divine goodness~~

12 ~~to the whole world; which you have redeemed through the grace of Christ our Savior.~~

Line 1. A very minor matter, but English teachers will notice and get distracted. While in countries that use the British form of spelling *judgement* is correct, in the U.S.A. the first *e* is deleted. As Winston Churchill observed wryly: "The United States and the United Kingdom are two great nations divided by a common language."

Line 1. A major matter. Theologically it is well to state that God is characterized both by judgment and compassion. Or as the traditional prayer quoted above puts it, God is both almighty and most merciful. Because in the past divine judgment was sometimes overemphasized to the point of making God seem to be a severe law enforcement agent, our age has overreacted by making God into a kind of celestial "wimp" who is unwilling to hold anyone accountable for anything. The truth surely lies in between.

Lines 1-4. This sentence is an example of structure that is too complex to be read in unison. Some simplification can be made by taking out unneeded phrases: "we know that" and "will and" (when "will" has just been stated in the previous clause). But beyond that, the sentence needs to be divided into several sentences. The phrase "the parental call" sounds more like something out of a textbook than a prayer book. The use of the phrases "heard your call" and "we hide from you" is intended to bring to mind the story of Adam and Eve who heard God's call in Eden and hid themselves. As is the case with almost all literary allusions, not everyone can be expected to "catch it"; but for those who do, the wording appropriately brings to mind the ancient saga of rebellion at the dawn of human existence.

Lines 4-8. Again, sentence structure can be simplified for ease in unison reading. Alternatively, the whole thing can be rearranged to read in this way: "You have called us to set before the world an example of your goodness. But we have failed. We have been selfish rather than gracious."

Lines 6-8. There will be present those who have given sacrificially of their time and energy to help family and friends; there will be those in the congregation who have faithfully prayed, studied the Scriptures, and tithed. They should not be asked to make an insincere confession. Perhaps these are the author's own sins, which certainly need to be confessed to God in private. But this language may also constitute what I call "preaching while praying"—a misdirected form of exhortation to the congregation to do better. If this kind of material is appropriate at all, it should be cast in provisional language: "If we have shown insufficient concern for our families and friends, forgive us. For times when we have neglected the disciplines of daily prayer and Bible reading, have mercy upon us. . . ."

Line 8. "Quality of magnanimity" is a phrase no congregation should ever be asked to utter aloud. It is the religious equivalent of "Many mighty men made music merrily." Even if it were more easily said, "magnanimity" is one of those words whose meaning many people know when they hear it, but would never use in a conversation. Hence its occurrence in unison prayer may seem artificial.

Lines 9-12. At line 9 the prayer of confession gets derailed, but so subtly we can easily miss what is happening. After all, is it not noble to pray for those whom we have offended? Certainly! But here petition for others becomes a diversionary tactic to get us sinners off the hook. As anyone who has given any attention to the skill of arguing knows, the best way to wiggle out of a corner is to change the subject. So here we stop confessing our sins and start praying for others. Ironically, we thereby add yet one more sin (evasion) to our already large collection of misdeeds! Worse yet, in this entire section there is nothing that suggests amendment of life. The prayer never gets around to asking God to give us the power to change our ways. Thus it does not do the complete work that is proper to a prayer of confession.

Below is a rewritten prayer that includes the editing explained above, together with a new ending.

God of judgment and compassion:
Look upon us with mercy.
You have called us to do you will,
  but we have ignored your ways.

We are like rebellious children.
We have heard your call,
  but we have run in the opposite direction.
We hide from you,
  rather than doing what you ask.
You have called us to set before the world
  an example of your goodness.

But we have failed.
We have been selfish rather than gracious.
Take from us our habit of disobedience.
Give us instead faithful hearts,
  that we may heed your word
   and do your work in the world
     as a testimony to your goodness.
As you have redeemed us,
  so also make us holy,
    through the grace of Christ our Savior.

Now two comments about how to put a unison prayer on the printed page of a church bulletin.

1. Note that instead of being printed margin to margin, above the prayer is printed in "sense lines." We have been using sense lines for many prayers in this book already; hence you know the form, even if you have not had a title for it. Most contemporary denominational books of worship use sense lines freely, especially for those things spoken in unison. The goal is to provide text of a narrow width so that the eye flows down the page. When the line of type is wider, the eye flows across the page; then sometimes when moving to the next line, the eye gets lost and ends up at the wrong place. Worshipers who find themselves saying the wrong words aloud tend to become embarrassed into silence, lest they make another mistake of this kind. The goal is to create a downward stream of vision that follows grammatical structure. Each full sentence starts at the left edge; but the remaining parts of the sentence are indented. This helps readers know how to say the phrases with meaning, and when to pause. Parallel constructions can be "stacked" one under the other (as in the prayer attributed to Saint Francis) in interlude B.

2. The second characteristic of prayers printed for congregational use is that the print style is that most usual to the eye, technically known as *lower case. Uppercase*, by contrast, uses only what are commonly called capital letters. Beause capital letters are larger than small letters, often it is incorrectly assumed they are more easily read; hence, it is very common in church bulletins to see the prayer above in this form:

GOD OF JUDGMENT AND COMPASSION: LOOK UPON US WITH YOUR MERCY.
YOU HAVE CALLED US TO DO YOUR WILL, BUT WE HAVE IGNORED YOUR
WAYS. WE ARE LIKE REBELLIOUS CHILDREN. WE HAVE HEARD YOUR CALL. . . .

But bigger is not always better. In lowercase, exactly half the letters of the English alphabet go fully above the line (*b, d, f, h, k, l*), partially above the line (*i, t*), below the line (*g, p, q, y*), or both below and partially above (*j*). These ascenders and descenders, as they are called, form word contours; our brains memorize these distinctive shapes. The dots of the *i* and *j* also help us recognize these two letters in lowercase, but are absent in uppercase. Using all upper-case destroys these contours and confuses the brain. Note the difference in the contours of the same words:

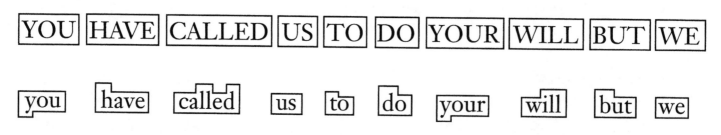

Can you see why material to be read in unison normally should appear in lowercase type?

On the Holiness of God

Read Job 38:1-24 and 39:19-40:5.

We have spoken about the boldness and freedom with which Christians may come before God, making requests as a child would of a human parent. For this there is clear warrant in the Bible. But it is only half of the story. The God to whom we come never ceases to be the Almighty and Eternal One. We, by contrast, are frail and mortal. Scripture provides a helpful alternation of these apparent opposites of the intimacy we have with God and the reverence due to God. This alternation, rightly observed, keeps us from falling into one extreme or the other: Without this, we may have a God who is so familiar as to be taken for granted or treated casually, or we may have a God who is so exalted as to be unapproachable. Neither will do.

The alternation is found in the opening words of the Lord's Prayer itself. "Our Father" suggests the closeness we may have with God. It may well be that Jesus, who spoke Aramaic (not Greek, in which the New Testament was written) at that point used the Aramaic term for God, which was used by him in Mark 14:36, and used by Paul in Romans 8:15 and Galatians 4:6. That word untranslated is "*abba*," somewhat the equivalent of the English "daddy." It is the most personal and affectionate name a child could use for a male parent. But having given us permission to be this familiar with God, Jesus immediately adds: "Hallowed be your name." Alternatively, this could be translated, "Holy is your name."

Holiness here has less to do with God's goodness than with God's separateness, with the distinctiveness of divine character. God is our maker, and the Creator is always far greater in understanding and power than the creature can be. That is the point of God's speech to Job, which you read at the beginning of this exercise. The gist of that word to Job is "How dare you suppose that you can understand me in detail!" It is the sentiment expressed in Isaiah 55:9 when God says, "For as the heavens are high above the earth, so are my ways higher than your ways and my thoughts than your thoughts."

In the Hebrew Scriptures there are many names for God, and a number of them point to the holiness or distinctive nature of the One who is worshiped. But set apart from all others is the name of God given to Moses at the burning bush in Exodus 3—that name rendered into English so strangely as "I AM," and then expanded upon even more mystifyingly as "I AM WHO I AM." We should be put on notice that this is no ordinary name by the fact that in many English translations it is set in all uppercase [capital] letters, as in the lines above. It is important to understand what is meant by these odd phrases, for they have to do with the holiness of God; and probably when Jesus says "Hallowed be your name," it is this particular name he has in mind.

Mentally Moses was comparing this God who appeared to him with the deities he had known growing up in the courts of Pharaoh. Egypt and the other nations surrounding the Hebrew peoples had multiple deities. Each had its own jurisdiction, which could be determined by its name. The Lord of the Rivers controlled the streams, but had no power over the birds of the air. The Ruler of the Stars had jurisdiction over the heavens, but had no authority over the grain fields. The Mistress of the Grain Harvest had nothing to say about the cattle. And so on. Each deity operated in its own box, so to speak. Each was limited by its title. But God says to Moses, "I am not one of these idols. I am not the result of human imagination. I exist. And beyond that do not try to understand me, much less limit me. I am the Creator and have jurisdiction over all things, not just over some things." Therein lies the holiness of God in the Bible. God is unlike any of us, and certainly unlike any of the idols we might construct.

So seriously did Jewish theology take this matter, that the Hebrew name given to Moses at the bush [YHWH] came to be regarded as unutterable. When the scriptures were read aloud, that most holy name was not pronounced; another title was substituted for it in speech. Because in Hebrew only consonants are written out and vowels are deleted, we do not even know how the original pronunciation might have sounded, had it been spoken aloud. The best guess is the form "Yahweh."

Here are two indications of this reverence for God's highest name in our own day.

1. In many English translations the secondary Hebrew title for God [*Adonai*] appears in print as "Lord," with an upper case opening letter and lower case letters thereafter. But since in spoken Hebrew *Adonai* was the name substituted for *YHWH*, wherever the most sacred name is found in the Hebrew, in English it is printed differently: the LORD. (Note the large upper case initial letter, with subsequent letters in smaller upper case, not lower case.) This is the pattern followed by the 1611 Authorized Version [King James], the *Revised Standard Version*, the *New Revised Standard Version*, the *New International Version*, and others. *The New English Bible* and the *Revised English Bible* go a step further by using uppercase type even for the definite article [the] that precedes: THE LORD. Thus the reader of any of these English translations can tell just by looking at the page that Psalm 23, for example, begins in Hebrew with *YHWH*, while Psalm 90 begins with the less exalted title "*Adonai*."

2. Many devout Jews when writing or typing the English word *God* will make it appear as *G-d*; the absent vowel creates an unpronounceable word, which may be read aloud as "the Holy One" or "the Almighty."

All of this reverence for the most holy name of God was in place in the time of Jesus. And it is likely that when he said "Let your name be holy" he meant the name revealed to Moses. This then sets up that important tension referred to above. On the one hand, we can call God by the most familiar title addressed to a loving human parent—*abba*, "our father" or even "daddy"; on the other hand, God is to be revered above all, by a name too sacred to be uttered by the human tongue.

Such tension (or alternation of seeming opposites) is a clue to much else that characterizes healthy thinking about God. Is God characterized by justice or by mercy? The most profound answer does not make a choice between these, but answers simply, "Yes." Is God further from us than the farthest star in the universe, or is God closer than our hands and feet and breathing? Again, the answer is "Yes." We do not choose between these opposites, but by holding them both in mind we can have a more biblical understanding of God.

Having thus far in these exercises stressed our boldness before God, we now need to add to that the necessity of deep reverence and awe. Not every prayer can do everything. So the kinds of prayers used earlier are quite legitimate. But in the course of the life of a congregation, they need to be balanced by the type of prayer we are considering in this exercise.

In part, the holiness of God is expressed by the words we choose to use, and in part by the words we choose to omit. Even our tone of voice or posture may be important. If the sound of the voice is too casual, the God to whom we pray may seem to be regarded more as the neighbor next door than the Maker of all things. One person who heard I was writing this book advised, "Please tell them not to slouch over the furniture when they pray." Obviously this person is distracted when the body of the prayer leader is draped casually over a lectern or kneeling bench (prayer desk, prie-dieu). Both words and bodily appearance can seem to connote a lack of respect for God's holiness. If these seem extreme responses, imagine how we would react if we saw on television a chief of state formally presenting a citation of honor to a citizen who repeatedly slapped the head of the nation on the back and said, "Well now, I sure do 'preciate what you're doin' here for me today, pardner." Likely many of us would prefer such scenes to be relegated to television reruns of *The Beverly Hillbillies*, not enacted in real life.

For the use of appropriate vocabulary that respects God's holiness, we do well to master the language of Scripture. The Psalms and poetic portions of books such as Isaiah are worth studying in detail, as are the acts of praise in the Revelation. But the whole of the Bible exudes a reverent respect for the God whom we worship.

This brings us to a troublesome practice of recent origin that is so widespread and accepted as normal that the mere mention of it will cause puzzlement to some people and consternation in others. I refer to the use of the word *just*, as in "We just ask your blessing, Lord." As there is widespread acceptance of this term in some quarters, there is in other places a revulsion against it—particularly when other set words accompany it, as in "We just want to." A particular name (derived from a characteristic casual pronunciation) has been given to this usage by those who dislike it. Many people, upon hearing I was writing this book, said, "I certainly hope you are going to talk about 'the weejuswanna' prayer." So what's the problem?

First, there is no biblical precedent for the use of this term *just* in this sense. When the Bible uses *just*, usually it is making reference to justice, as in Psalm 119:121: "I have done what is just and right." Indeed in the full complex of prayers in the book of Psalms, the NRSV uses the word *just* only six times; never is it used there in the sense of "We just come to you. . . ." When the word is not used to connote justice, it may indicate immediacy ("Just as Jesus was getting into the boat") or comparison ("I am such a person, just as you are.") Never in a reputable English translation of Scripture do we find the phrase "we just want to." Nor is *just* used in any of the standard prayers of the ages in the way that has become so widespread in the last few decades. To many persons who cherish the Scriptures and the prayers of the centuries, "the weejuswanna prayer" is an unwelcome intruder, a newcomer that jars the ears. Its use may even seem to some to connote ignorance of, or even a certain contempt for, biblical language patterns.

Second, the recently pervasive prayer phrase connotes to many people an undue casualness; for these who wish to join you in prayer, " the weejuswanna prayer" is the oral equivalent of draping your body over the church furniture. In order to understand why, consider how we choose our words in ordinary conversation. I may well knock on the door of my next-door neighbor and then begin our conversation by saying, "I just want to tell you that I am going to be out of town for a few days. I'm taking the limo to the airport, so my car will always be in the driveway." The *just* here appropriately suggests that this is no big deal. I am not asking the neighbor to bring in my mail or water my plants; I only want to prevent undue alarm in my neighbor's mind when my car does not move from my driveway for several days. There is no need to call the police to investigate whether I am dead or disabled in my house. The neighbors now know that I am "just" out of town on a planned trip. In that context, the use of the word *just* is very appropriate. But never would I knock on my neighbor's door to announce: "I just came over to tell you your dog has been struck by a car and appears to be dead." There the word *just* suggests that I care little about the dog and less about my neighbor's grief. If I am forced to make such a sad announcement, my opening words more likely will be, "I am very sorry to have to bring you such bad news, but your dog has been struck."

Words have significance, and to people who have been schooled in the language of the Bible and the historic forms of prayer, "We just" appears to mean: "This prayer is no big deal, God. And, by the way, maybe you're not such a big deal yourself." Almost never is such a lack of reverence intended by the leader of prayer. "The weejuswanna prayer" has become so ubiquitous as to be unquestioned in some circles. But many people will perceive disrespect for God to exist, intended or not. Your choice of language will distract such persons rather than accomplish your task, which is to hold their attention to the act of praying. Even in those circles where the use of *just* is readily accepted, it is unlikely that this word will be missed if you neglect to use it—especially if the worshipers are familiar with the vocabulary of prayer in Scripture. So consider calling a moratorium on the usage. The whole church, not only a portion of it, needs to be able to say "Amen!"

As I have done before, I commend to you the prayers of the Bible. Except for its Christian closing, the following prayer of adoration is drawn entirely from the Psalms, sometimes directly and at other points paraphrased or adapted for the sake of clarity to those who will say the amen.

> *We have heard with our ears, O God,*
> > *our ancestors have told us*
> > *what deeds you performed in their days.*   (44:1-2)
> *You are our refuge and strength,*
> > *a well proved help in trouble*   (46:1)
> *How great are your works.*
> *Your thoughts are very deep.*   (92:5)
> *Every day we bless you*
> > *and praise your name for ever and ever.*
> *You are gracious and merciful,*
> > *slow to anger, and abounding in steadfast love.*
> *You are good to all,*
> > *and your compassion is over all that you have made.*   (145:1-2, 8-9)
> *You alone are God.*   (86:10*b*)
> *You have turned our mourning into dancing;*
> *you have taken off our sackcloth and clothed us with joy.*
> *Therefore we praise you and cannot be silent.*   (30:11-12)

You are the hope of all the ends of the earth
*   and of the farthest seas.*   (65:5)
Be exalted, O God, above the heavens.
Let your glory be over all the earth;   (57:11)
This we pray through the power and presence of Jesus Christ our Savior.

Note that this is a prayer of pure adoration and praise. No petitions are made except to ask at the very end that God's glory may shine above the heavens and cover the whole earth. Even that is more a form of praise than a request. Because there are no petitions, the verbs are not vigorous; the content is in adjectives and adverbs. The primary verb is the *are* that accompanies the *you* and *your* addressed to God. In such a prayer, then, the challenge to the author is to use a variety of descriptive words, with as little repetition as possible.

As a way of reviewing the collect form, consider how easily such a prayer can be constructed on the basis of a Psalm portion.

Psalm 108:5-6

Be exalted, O God, above the heavens,
   and let your glory be over all the earth.
Give victory with your right hand, and answer me,
   so that those whom you love may be rescued.

Collect based on Psalm 108:5-6

O God,
you are exalted above the heavens, and your glory is over all the earth.
Give victory with your right hand, and answer us,
so that those whom you love may be rescued;
through Jesus Christ our victorious Savior.

Here, of course, there is a petition; it is not possible to have a collect without one. Even so, the emphasis of the prayer is on the goodness of the God who can be counted on to help those who are in need.

Now we turn to the task of editing the text of a prayer intended to focus on the praise of the holy God.

1   Dear God: How great are your gifts to us and to all of your children. For all that you have given

2   to us, we just want to bless your holy name. You have created all things, and we know that you

3   are the ruler of everything that exists, Oh Holy One. Great is thy faithfulness; thy promises are

4   trustworthy. Before you every knee shall bow, for we are reminded that you are our maker and

5   there is none other like you. We just praise you. We offer you our lives in faithful service. We

6   want you to save us from supposing we know more about you than mortals can know. Just save

7   us from that. Nevertheless, enable us to seek your will, lest we fail to discern what we can

8   come to know through your grace. By your greatness and strength, undergird us. By your love

9   and faithfulness, protect us. By your wisdom and power direct us in all we do, so that we may

10   proclaim your wonderful works to all who wish to see. Let us reflect the brightness of God's

11   glory in every word and action. For the goodness of the Lord is worthy to be sung in all the

12   earth. All praise to you, O Triune God, in every place, by every creature, now and through all

13   ages.

Do not proceed to the next page until you have completed your editing of the prayer above.

Suggested Revisions and Commentary

           Glorious

1   ~~Dear~~ God: How great are your gifts to us and to all of your children. For all that you have given

2   to us, we ~~just want to~~ bless your holy name. You have created all things, and ~~we know that~~ you

                            O   your   your

3   are the ruler of everything that exists, ~~Oh~~ Holy One. Great is ~~thy~~ faithfulness; ~~thy~~ promises are

4   trustworthy. Before you every knee shall bow, for ~~we are reminded that~~ you are our maker; and

5   there is none other like you. We ~~just~~ praise you. We offer you our lives in faithful service. ~~We~~

                    Save

6   ~~want you to save~~ us from supposing we know more about you than mortals can know. ~~Just save~~

7   ~~us from that.~~ Nevertheless, enable us to seek your will, lest we fail to discern what we can

8   come to know through your grace. By your greatness and strength, undergird us. By your love

9   and faithfulness, protect us. By your wisdom and power direct us in all we do, so that we may

                                        Cause us to reflect your

10   proclaim your wonderful works to all who wish to see. ~~Let us reflect the brightness of God's~~

                        your

11   glory in every word and action. For ~~the~~ goodness ~~of the Lord~~ is worthy to be sung in all the

12   earth. All praise to you, O Triune God, in every place, by every creature, now and through

13   all ages.

Line 1. *Dear* is in certain circles a controversial word when addressed to God. To some people it seems overly chummy, as in "my dear pal." (John Wesley was of this mind, but his brother, Charles, was not. In "O For a Thousand Tongues to Sing," Charles wrote of "my dear Redeemer's praise." That is how many non-Methodists sing it to this day. But John detested what he considered to be unduly familiar language for God; so he changed the phrase to "my great Redeemer's praise," and Methodists have always used John's alteration.) In what may seem to be a contradictory opinion, others regard *dear* as being unduly lacking in warmth because it seems too reminiscent of the opening of a business letter. Personally, I do not hold strongly to either objection; but for the sake of those who do, I almost never use *dear* as a form of address in public prayer. Particularly when emphasizing the holiness of God, something more exalted seems in order. "Glorious" is by no means the only possible alternative. Consider "Most Righteous God," "Ruler of the Universe," or "Almighty and Eternal One." "Holy God" would work, were it not for the fact that the sentence ends with a reference to "your holy name"; the same word should not be used at both ends of the sentence when plenty of other words are available.

Line 3. When a prayer is spoken, the difference between *O* and *oh* cannot be distinguished. But in print it is a very different matter. *O* is called "the vocative," referring to the use of the voice to get someone's attention. For example, suppose I see John at some distance down the hallway and call out, "O John," to let him know that I would like to speak with him. That is the vocative *O*. *Oh* is called "the expressive," because it expresses a certain emotion, be it surprise, disappointment, or sorrow. Examples; "Oh! Jane, you startled me." "Oh, Bill! I am so distressed at the poor job you did." "Oh, Tanya, I'm sorry to hear your mother is ill." Note also the difference in punctuation. In the vocative there is no punctuation inserted between the *O* and the name being called. But the *oh* expressive usually is followed by a comma or an exclamation mark. In prayer, God is almost universally addressed by the vocative, not the expressive. I use the following to try to help my students remember the difference: On Monday morning, the Christian awakes and happily sings, "O God, another day in which to do your work." But the secularist awakes and grumbles, "Oh, god! Another work day!"

Line 3. Those who know older translations of Scripture (or even a hymn stanza, as in this case) readily slip out of contemporary English into the earlier forms. In extempore prayer, it will happen. Don't worry about it. But check written prayers for consistency of expression. The more you do this, the lest apt you will be to flit between *your* and *thy*, even when praying without preparation.

Lines 6-7. Some of the deletions in this prayer I make no comments about. The reason for their removal is obvious by now. But "Just save us from that" not only contains the *just* word; the entire sentence says nothing we have not said in the previous sentence. Vain repetition!

Lines 8-10. Here I have set up three parallel structures: "By your _____, do this. . . ." The third one is expanded with a purpose, first learned in the collect form. The six attributes of God, two in each sentence, constitute another way of praising the holy God.

Lines 10-11. Here the prayer slips into talking to the congregation and talking about God rather than to God. Keep the language of prayer on the track.

Now write a prayer of adoration of your own. For ideas, turn to the Psalms of praise. The better you know the language of the Bible, the easier this task will be—and the more it will strike chords that resonate inside those who pray with you.

Prayer of Adoration

_____

_____

_____

_____

_____

_____

_____

_____

_____

_____

_____

_____

_____

_____

_____

_____

_____

_____

_____

_____

When you have finished your draft, check the following:
1. In places where you relied on the Psalms, how closely did you follow their use of language?
2. Is the prayer pure adoration and praise, or did you inadvertently slip into confession or petition?
3. Are there strong descriptive words throughout?
4. Is there a good variety of language, or are the same words used again and again?
5. Is the prayer crisp and lacking in words that do no work, particularly in phrases such as "we just want to. . . ."?
Revise your draft as necessary.

Then look over the prayer of adoration you wrote in exercise 1. I think you will see how greatly your sensitivity to language has increased and how your writing skills have developed since the first exercise.

Praying to the God Who Is Present

Read Psalm 8.

Given the seriousness and extent of human sin, and given the grandeur and scope of the work of the Holy God, it could readily be supposed that so magnificent a deity hardly has time to notice what occurs on planet earth, this tiny orb on the edge of one galaxy among multitudes of galaxies. It could be so supposed, and we would not be the first to have such thoughts. Even when the universe appeared to human eyes to be far smaller than we know it to be, the Psalmist wrote:

> O LORD, our Sovereign,
>   how majestic is your name in all the earth!
> When I look at your heavens, the work of your fingers,
>   the moon and the stars that you have established,
> what are human beings that you are mindful of them,
>   mortals that you care for them?

Yet neither our smallness in comparison to the vastness of the universe nor our sin caused the Hebrew poet to conclude that God has no interest in human beings. On the contrary, the Psalmist continued:

> Yet you have made them a little lower than God,
>   and crowned them with glory and honor. (Psalm 8:1, 3-5)

The Psalmist strongly affirmed that God is at work in our midst, fully engaged in our destiny. In contrast, sometimes Christian prayer seems to suggest that God is disinterested, distant, even absent. This is not intended by those who offer the prayers; it is the result of too little consideration of what is being said. A combination of bad habits in prayer conspires to create what can be called "The Absent Deity Syndrome." In medicine, a syndrome is a combination of symptoms, which, taken together, point to a particular illness. So also in prayer: A combination of ways of talking to God can point to a seeming lack of conviction that God is in our midst, ever concerned for our welfare. Such a lack of conviction is indeed a kind of spiritual illness.

We have already considered separately most of the symptoms that constitute the syndrome. Now we need to look at them in combination, for when used together they reinforce each other in unfortunate ways.

1. When we ask God to "be with" one person or another, we imply that God normally is *not* with us. This is contrary to nature of Jesus who is Emmanuel—"God with us." It ignores the promise of Jesus to assemblies of his people that "Where two or three are gathered in my name, I am there among them" (Matt. 18:20). It also overlooks his final assurance to be with us to the end of time (Matt. 28:20). Recall our discussion of this matter in exercise 5. Note that Jesus did not say he would be present among us only if we invite him.

2. An intensification of the suggestion that God is absent occurs if, at the beginning of a service of worship, we ask God to "come and be present in our midst." Sometimes this kind of prayer is even given a name that complicates the problem. For the term *invocation* means "calling in." If we have to call God in, obviously we imply God is not already in our midst.

At times we properly ask the God who is present to act in a particular way; we invoke the power of the Holy Spirit to bless the bread and cup at Communion, for example, and this may properly be called "the invocation of the Spirit." But asking the present God to grant a particular blessing is not the same as asking God to be present, as if God were usually absent from us. What is customarily called "the invocation" is better replaced with a "prayer of adoration" of the type discussed in exercise 10.

3. If we address God by name again and again, this can seem to suggest that God, if not totally absent, at least has a short attention span; therefore we must keep trying to get (or hold) God's interest in our prayer. Recall that in the Lord's Prayer, Jesus addressed God by name only once. In a long prayer additional addresses to God may well be appropriate, but in general follow the rule that "less is more." In exercise 6, we looked at this matter of using God's name too frequently, and we do well to review it here.

This facet of the syndrome has to do not only with the number of times God is addressed but also with the lack of variety in the forms of address. Eight consecutive uses of the term *Lord* will do more to suggest God is inattentive than will addressing God in varying ways: Lord, Guardian, Shepherd, Redeemer, Friend, Sovereign, Rock of Salvation, and Guide.

4. We further suggest God is absent when in prayer we talk *about* rather than *to* God, as in "We trust in God's love" rather than "We trust in your love." We noted this in exercise 5.

5. Certain phrases seem to address the congregation instead of God. We have also noted this when talking about a tendency to say "let us" and "may we" instead of addressing vigorous verbs to God. See exercise 5. The language of exhortation to the people should never be substituted for the language of petition to God when we are at prayer.

6. Finally there is the problem of the pesky verb *might*, as in "Grant that we might. . . ." This word has two uses: First, *might* is the past tense of *may*.

Present tense: We hope that he may visit us.

Past tense: We had hoped that she might have visited us.

In the past tense *might* can be used without giving it a second thought.

But the present tense is trickier. There *might* suggests at least a tinge of doubt in comparison to its companion word *may*. If I say "I might do that," I imply that I am less likely to do it than if I say, "I may do that." To put it another way, *might* suggests *might not* in a way that *may* does not suggest *may not*. Often in prayer *might* inappropriately turns up in the purpose attached to a petition. For example: "Direct us in our search for truth, that we might walk in your way."

What we may seem to be saying is that we are really not so sure we will be given enough divine guidance to walk in God's way. When taken in combination with items 1-5, the use of *might* in the present tense further suggests that God is not fully engaged in answering our prayers. Therefore the verb of the purpose clause should always be *may* not *might*.

To make it as simple as possible: When in doubt, use the verb *may* unless you are dealing with something in the past.

Any one of these six symptoms encountered alone may cause little difficulty. But if they gang up and occur side-by-side in the same prayer, the not-so-hidden message seems to be, "We are not really convinced God is paying attention to us, or even cares about us." Then we appear to be imploring an absent God rather than one who not only is present and reaches out to us even before we utter a word. Once more, almost never does a leader of prayer intend to convey such a negative message about God. But if we do not choose our language carefully, such a signal will be sent to the worshipers in spite of our good intentions.

So suppose now that you are asked to edit a "Prayer of Invocation" for the beginning of a Sunday service. How will you improve the following?

Granted, what follows is an extreme example of "The Absent Deity Syndrome." (At times exaggeration is a useful teaching tool!) All of these things do occur in public prayer with some regularity, however. So consider how this can be rewritten in order to be an opening prayer that acknowledges God's presence rather than pleading for it.

1   Oh God, as we gather together in this time of worship, we ask you to be here in our midst.

2   Although we are unworthy of your presence, God, just come into our congregation in spite of

3   our sin. Let us look for God's presence among us as the scriptures are read and interpreted to us.

4   And may we keep our attention on what we are taught about the Lord. We remember all who

5   cannot attend today. We just want to ask you to be with them, Father. And, Father, especially

6   be present with those who suffer great pain due to sickness or sorrow. Let us do what we can to

7   support and encourage them, to show them God's love. Now, Lord, we thank you for coming

8   into our midst today, if it is your will. Grant that we might be ever greatful for our blessings,

9   lest we take divine goodness for granted. And we will be careful to give God the glory in all

10 things for Jesus' sake.

Do not proceed to the next page until you have completed the editing of the prayer above.

Suggested Revisions and Commentary

1   O God,   we give thanks that you are ever with us.
    ~~Oh God, as we gather together~~ in this time of worship, ~~we ask you to be here in our midst.~~

    Despite our sinfulness, you are always eager to make your forgiving and transforming presence
2   ~~Although we are unworthy of your presence, God, just come into our congregation in spite of~~

    known. By the power of your Holy Spirit, enable us to discover you
3   ~~our sin. Let us look for God's presence~~ among us as the scriptures are read and interpreted to us.

    Focus our minds upon   you.   Reveal your goodness to
4   ~~And may we keep our attention on~~ what we are taught about ~~the Lord~~. ~~We remember~~ all who

                      Strengthen and sustain them.   Especially minister
5   cannot attend today. ~~We just want to ask you to be with them, Father. And Father, especially~~

    graciously and tenderly to   Teach us how   best
6   ~~be present with~~ those who suffer great pain due to sickness or sorrow. ~~Let us do what~~ we can ~~to~~

                                                          your   We thank you for your presence in
7   support and encourage them, to show them ~~God's~~ love. ~~Now, Lord, we thank you for coming~~

                      Enable us always to be grateful for all you give us,
8   ~~into~~ our midst. ~~today, if it is your will. Grant the we might be ever greatful for our blessings,~~

              your   teach us to glorify you
9   lest we take ~~divine~~ goodness for granted. And ~~we will be careful to give God the glory~~ in all

10 things, for Jesus' sake.

I have revised this text quite extensively. I do not expect you will have edited it as thoroughly or in precisely the same way, but did you at least identify the same problems in the text?

Line 1. Remember the difference between "O God" and "Oh God"? If not, refer to exercise 10. My deletion of "as we gather together" is an illustration of personal discretion in editing. This is not inflated language or useless verbiage. Were it left in, no harm would be done. Its inclusion or deletion is a matter of personal judgment—unlike "we ask you to be here in our midst." The latter phrase suggests that God is not here and is misleading at best and heretical at worst in the light of Matthew 18:20.

Line 2. Rather than beginning the sentence with an admission of unworthiness and ending it with another reference to sin, I choose to begin with "despite our sinfulness" and then in the middle to insert "forgiving and transforming" as a more positive approach to how God deals with sinners.

Lines 3-5. From "Let us look" through "cannot attend today" there is no verb of petition, and God is referred to twice in the third person. Hence these are statements that could be made to the congregation, not prayers to the Almighty. We do again begin to speak to God in line 5, but with the suggestion that God may be absent from the lives of those for whom we pray. Reasons for my revisions should be evident.

Line 6. Two-thirds of the way through, we return to exhortation and to talking about God.

Lines 7-8. Even the revised "we thank you for your presence in our midst" could be further edited, since it says nothing new. But some repetition in prayer is tolerable. I do choose to remove the word *today* in line 8. It is not a major problem, but can tend to reinforce the notion that God is present at some times and not at others. In line 8 is another of those matters that will trouble no one unless the text of the prayer is printed out; but then good spellers will remind you that *greatful* is not an English word.

Now a postscript. Within this book I regularly suggest using biblical prayers as models for our own prayer. Yet often biblical prayers—particularly the Psalms—do precisely what I have cautioned against above. They talk to God and about God alternatively. Consider, for example, Psalm 9:1-10. The opening line talks about God: "I will give thanks to the LORD." The next line talks to God: "I will tell of all your wonderful works." The psalmist continues to address God in the second person until verse 7, then jumps back to the third person: "But the LORD sits enthroned forever." In verse 10 the psalmist again talks to God: "And those who know your name put their trust in you." So how do I defend my position?

In the biblical understanding of things, God is equally praised through direct address and through a narration of divine goodness and action. To move from one grammatical form to the other is acceptable and, as a literary style, provides variety. Early Christian prayer followed the same patterns, as is seen in many Prayers of Thanksgiving at the Lord's Supper. We typically begin those prayers by addressing God directly in praise and petition. Then we move into the narrative of events at Jesus' meals with his followers and talk about what he did while at table: "On the same night in which he was betrayed and arrested. . . ." Then we move back to petitioning God: "Send the power of the Holy Spirit upon us and upon this bread and cup." Such alternation is thoroughly biblical, and all of it is regarded as prayer.

Herein lies the problem for us: We have moved so far away from this particular biblical pattern that to use it often engenders confusion. Many people who are attentive to grammatical structure do indeed ask concerning the eucharistic prayer: "Why is it that we *stop praying* in the middle of the prayer and later start in again?" Unlike people in biblical times, our religious culture does not seem to understand that narrating God's goodness is an alternative way of addressing prayer to God.

Given this change in understanding, it is better not to confuse worshipers by making such shifts if the shifts are not necessary. (The use of the "words of institution" is so fixed in eucharistic tradition that the story about Jesus taking bread, giving thanks, breaking, and distributing it is necessarily retained.) Because I teach in a theological seminary, when I am asked the question about why "we stop praying," usually it is by seminary students; most of them have had some background in biblical studies and should be better able to grasp what is going on than laity who have never take a course in the Psalms or the biblical tradition of prayer. Hence the basis of my advice not to alternate between second and third person is based on practical issues of our own time, not on biblical precedent or theological understanding.

Exercise 12

Praying to the Trinity

Read Matthew 28:16-20.

A classic understanding of the Triune God advises us of four crucial principles:

    1. God is eternally Father, Son, and Holy Spirit.
    2. The Father is God.
       The Son is God.
       The Holy Spirit is God.
    3. The Father is neither the Son nor the Holy Spirit.
       The Son is neither the Father nor the Holy Spirit.
       The Holy Spirit is neither the Father nor the Son.
    4. Yet there are not three gods but One God, who is eternal and undivided.

As complex and confusing as all of that may seem (particularly if you have never set foot inside a theological seminary), all of it is crucial to the church's historic understanding of God. Therefore, the failure to bear this statement in mind can result in a very confused interpretation of the Christian faith. It can even result in tritheism: the worship of three separate deities.

Consider the kinds of confused phrases that get dropped into prayers without much thought, but which then teach congregations misleading ideas. For example: "Heavenly Father, we thank you that at Bethlehem you became human for us." This suggests a sequential understanding of the Trinity: God was Father from creation until Bethlehem; then God became the Son for about thirty years; finally God became the Holy Spirit and is so now. This may well seem to conform to principle 3 if taken alone. But principle 1 is thus violated—the Father did not become the Son or Spirit at any time but has been Father, Son, and Spirit eternally. (The eternal Son did become Jesus of Nazareth at a certain point, but that is a quite different matter.)

And things can get more complicated than that. For example, I once received from a student a prayer that began with the words "Heavenly Father." But very shortly into the prayer, and without additional address used, the prayer said, "We give you thanks that you died on the cross for us." The student had ignored the assertion that "The Son is neither the Father nor the Holy Spirit"; without knowing it the student had fallen into the ancient heresy of "patripassianism"—the idea that the Father died at Calvary.

This is not a textbook in trinitarian understanding, nor am I qualified to write such a volume. I simply want to alert you to how readily you can slip into what has historically been identified as heresy so that you will be cautious about how you use trinitarian language. But primarily I want to give you some guidance as to how to pray to the Trinity legitimately.

There are two reasonably easy ways of avoiding trinitarian difficulties in prayer:

1. Address a prayer to one of the Three Persons, and in the closing mention the other Persons:

Note here an address and a corresponding closing for each Person:

    (a) Heavenly Father . . .
       through Jesus Christ, who with you and the Holy Spirit lives and reigns,
       one God, for ever and ever.

(b) Blessed Jesus [or a christological title such as "Holy Savior" or "Son of God"] . . .
   who with the Father and the Spirit lives and reigns, one God, for ever and ever.
(c) Gracious Holy Spirit . . .
   through Jesus Christ, who with you and the Father lives and reigns, one God,
   for ever and ever.

There are other ways of phrasing the closings. For example, (a) could be phrased: through Jesus Christ our Savior, who lives and reigns with you in the unity of the Holy Spirit, now and for ever.

2. Frame the prayer in three consecutive segments of about the same length. Address the first to the Father, the second to the Son, and the third to the Spirit. Often such a prayer closes with a doxology such as "Blessed are you, Holy Trinity, One God, now and evermore."

For example:

Father of lights, in you is no variation or shadow of change.
You are the fount of every perfect gift,
   and the source of every generous act of giving.   James 1:17
You have adopted us as your children,   Ephesians 1:5
   and have made us a royal priesthood,
   calling us out of darkness into your marvelous light   1 Peter 2:9
Blessed are you now and forever!

Jesus Christ, Light of the world, and Word Eternal,   John 8:12; 1:1
   you illuminate everyone and everything.   John 1: 9
When the earth was cloaked in darkness at Calvary,
when the sun refused to shine,   Matthew 27:45
   you shone forth most brightly,
   and by your resurrection
      you hold all things together,   Colossians 1:17
      making peace by the blood of the cross.   Colossians 1:20
Blessed are you now and forever!

Holy Spirit, you have enlightened us
   and allowed us to taste the heavenly gift,   Hebrews 6:4
   that we may serve others with glad and generous hearts.   Acts 2:46
You freely pour out power upon your followers;   Acts 2:1-4, 17
You establish the church as a city set upon a hill,
   as a lamp on a lamp-stand,
      to give light to all within the house.   Matthew 5:14-15
Blessed are you now and forever!

Worthy are you, Holy and Undivided Trinity,
   of all blessing and glory and wisdom
and thanksgiving and honor and power and might
      for ever and ever!   Revelation 7:12

Note that this is entirely a prayer of praise to the Trinity. There are no requests made of God. Certainly it would be legitimate to organize a prayer of intercession around the Trinity; but in this instance I chose not to do so. I used parallel constructions as follows:
In each segment reference is made to an attribute of light in relation to that Person.
Each portion then goes on to indicate the work that characterizes this Person.
Each part ends with a common phrase, "Blessed are you now and forever."

The prayer concludes with the great doxology drawn from the Revelation.

Trinitarian prayer is not without its challenges quite apart from the four principles noted at the beginning of the exercise. In many circumstances there are those at prayer who have great difficulty with "Father" language, either because of personal difficulties with a male parent or because of more generalized practices related to patriarchal power and gender discrimination throughout the history of Judaism and Christianity. In such instances care must be taken to honor the experiences of such persons and to try gently to help them understand that, in the best of circumstances, "Father" is a metaphor, not an anatomical description. The first Person of the Trinity is no more a biological male because of being called "Father" than Jesus is a block of wood because of being called "the door" in John 10:7. Scripture calls God a rock and a fortress, under no illusions that the Almighty is an inert and inanimate object.

In general, it is better to deal with trinitarian language by addition than by deletion or substitution. To delete all reference to God as Father is to eviscerate much of Scripture and church tradition. However, the most popular substitutions are not equivalent to trinitarian terms. For example, "creator, redeemer, and sustainer" is not the same as "Father, Son, and Holy Spirit." The latter is relational language; it deals with Persons of God, of which there are only three revealed to us. The former is functional language; it deals with the acts of God, of which there are more known to us than we can count. God is shepherd, guide, judge, helper, ruler, defender, counselor, and on and on and on. Nor is any one function the exclusive prerogative of just one Person of the Trinity. The Father creates; the Son creates; the Spirit creates. The Father redeems; the Son redeems; the Spirit redeems; and so on.

At times, instead of "Father, Son, and Holy Spirit," phrases such as "Holy and Undivided Trinity" may be used, as I did at the conclusion of the prayer above. At other times (such as during baptism) the usual formula may be required by denominational law or the full weight of tradition, but something like this may be added to it: "The One who is the Mother of us all." To ears accustomed to exclusively male language for God, this may be jarring. But such ears are unfamiliar both with the language of the Bible and with the rich heritage of prayer across the centuries. Female language for God has been used by Jews and Christians, to the great edification of both of these communities of faith. For example, in Isaiah 42:14, God is compared to a woman in childbirth; and Jesus compares himself to a mother hen gathering her brood (Matt. 23:37).

Some recent forms of prayer with every good intention confuse matters. For example, there are now numerous collects that are addressed "O God" and then conclude "through Jesus Christ our Lord, who lives and reigns with you and the Holy Spirit." Traditionally such a prayer was addressed to the Father, and hence the trinitarian ending made sense. Obviously such prayers are now addressed to "God" in an effort to avoid "Father" language. But since the only antecedent for "you" is "O God," the logical interpretation of the prayer's meaning is that God lives and reigns with Christ and the Spirit. Wait a minute! Doesn't principle 2 above advise us that Christ *is* God and that the Spirit *is* God? The Father can live with the Son and the Spirit and still be one God (principle 3); but if God lives with God, doesn't that give us more than one God? Therefore I urgently avoid using a trinitarian closing when the address is a generic reference to God. The simpler closing "through Jesus Christ our Lord" causes fewer problems.

Much more thought together with open dialogue and intensive education will be needed in this area if we are to work our way out of the current impasse. During this time, care must be taken that prayer not become a battleground over these issues. This implies both careful preparation of the language used in prayer and equally careful interpretation of theology, fore and aft, to the praying community. The problems of appropriate trinitarian language will not go away, and churches committed to their heritage in the Christian tradition cannot ignore, let alone abolish, trinitarian understanding. But the wisdom of God has yet a long way to lead us before we know how to resolve the difficulties. In the interim, be aware of the issues, and when at prayer avoid the most obvious pitfalls.

Now try your hand at writing a prayer of each of the types discussed in detail above.

First, remind yourself of the five parts of the collect form. Then write a collect addressed to one person of the Trinity, and conclude with a trinitarian closing.

1. _____

2. _____

_____

3. _____

_____

4. _____

_____

5. _____

_____

When you have finished, check the address to be certain it is specific to one Person, not generically addressed to "God." Then check the closing to be sure it mentions the two Persons of the Trinity not named in the Address. Look at the prayer as a whole, checking its five parts and doing any necessary final editing.

Then write a longer prayer in three parts (plus a conclusion) addressed to each Person separately.

I. _____

_____

_____

_____

_____

_____

_____

_____

III. _____

_____

_____

_____

_____

_____

_____

III. _____

_____

_____

_____

_____

_____

_____

Conclusion—_____

Check the parts of the prayer to see if they are parallel in construction and approximately equal in length. Check the content of each part against the principles at the head of this exercise. Does any part violate any principle? If so, how can you alter it to avoid the difficulty? Does the conclusion draw the parts of the prayer together in a final trinitarian statement?

The Physical Aspects of Public Prayer

The physical space within which we pray can make an important contribution to the act of prayer itself. Some buildings seem inherently worshipful. Upon entering them, we feel a sense of awe or peace. Whether they are simple, ornate, or something in between, they invite prayer. Other spaces have an opposite effect. We have to strain to enter into meditation within them. As a leader of prayer, you may not be able to do much about the appearance and effect of the room; but you do well to know in advance what the physical situation is.

It will also be helpful for you to know any special characteristics of sound transmission within the room. Some buildings are very "live"—sound carries well in them and there is a long reverberation time. This is the kind of room musicians love. But speakers may need to exercise special care in the articulation of consonants, the separation of words, and the rate of speaking. "Slow down and make your tongue work hard" is the advice for this kind of setting. Other rooms are very "dry" or "dead." Reverberation time seems not to exist, and even the Mormon Tabernacle Choir would not sound good in the setting. In such a room careful attention needs to be given to maintaining volume and not cutting off vowel sounds too rapidly.

The extremes of the types of acoustical settings can almost be predicted by a visual inspection of the space. A wooden or stone floor, masonry walls, wooden ceiling, and absence of fabrics usually mean a live room. Carpeted floors, draperies, velour pew cushions, drywall panels, and—in the worst case scenario—acoustical tile on the ceiling almost infallibly indicate a room that renders sound dead on arrival. These architectural and decorative characteristics are beyond your power to change, but you can attempt to compensate for them.

Many rooms have mixed acoustical characteristics. Those who sit in different locations from week to week will tell you that they have discovered the "cold" and "hot" spots in the room. Sometimes pews that are perpetually avoided tell you that the entire congregation has caught on to places where the acoustics are poor. On the other hand, rooms with domed ceilings often have special acoustical properties that allow you to stand in a certain spot and be clearly heard at other points many feet away, even if you whisper. The more fully you can learn about the room in which you work, the more satisfactorily you can use your voice for the edification of all.

In many situations, the place within the worship area to be used by the leader of prayer is fixed not only by tradition but also by nails, bolts, and screws. There is, for example, one piece of furniture fastened to the floor, with a microphone permanently attached to it. The implication is: Stand here and nowhere but here. Or the room has one prie-dieu (prayer desk or kneeler) screwed to the floor. Kneel there or else. No thought has been given to the needs of someone who is to lead the prayers from a wheelchair, or even to the possibility that the prayer leader may be located at one place at a certain point during the service and somewhere else at a different time. So that is that, until you can convince the powers that be to renovate the space—which most likely won't happen next week.

But in other situations there will be choices; and when the renovation does occur, a primary consideration should be flexibility. A prayer of exaltation on a very joyous occasion may well be offered from a central point, with the leader whose hands are outstretched being unobscured by furniture. This positioning denotes freedom and joy. A unison prayer of confession on a penitential occasion may be led from a prie-dieu off to one side; the near invisibility of the leader stresses that all are equally sinners before God. During a litany, the prayer desk may be set within the center aisle, with the leader facing the same direction as the congregation rather than visually confronting the rest of the worshipers. The position reinforces the interactive nature of the litany form. If the litany is sung or chanted, the leader and musicians will need to be located such that they can see each other; thus subtle signals can be exchanged between them, as needed. A prayer immediately before or after a sermon probably will be given from the pulpit, while a prayer of thanksgiving over the bread and wine certainly will be said at the Lord's Table, as the prayer over the baptismal water will be spoken at the font. And so on. Ideally, there is no single spot from which prayer is to be led.

But variation in the placement of the leader of prayer should spring from a thoughtful rationale, not from an ill-considered hankering to "do something different this week because we have gotten into a rut." (Those who still remember the days of unpaved roads may recall that so long as they were not too deep, ruts could be very useful in making one's way through unfamiliar muddy terrain. Usually the ruts had been made by drivers who knew where stones and cinders had purposefully been embedded in the clay. It was getting out of the rut for no particularly good reason that was apt to land your vehicle in the quagmire!)

The thoughtful rationale may be related to a sense of occasion. Because Lent is a penitential season, it may be well to kneel for prayers during the season. But the Council of Nicaea (A.D. 325) forbade kneeling throughout the Great Fifty Days of Easter, noting that standing is the posture of resurrection. Hence standing for prayer at that time provides an important visual contrast between Lent and Easter. On the occasion of a great local or national tragedy, it may be well to kneel, while on a festive occasion such as the consecration of a new church building, standing may be more in keeping with the spirit of the day. Some prayers may be said from a sitting position, particularly in a meditative setting. If one or more of the leaders of worship is in a wheelchair, other leaders of worship may wish to remain seated also. Certainly in chapels of retirement and convalescent facilities, it may be well for the entire congregation to remain seated through the entire service.

Standing, sitting, and kneeling all are historic postures for prayer. But even more stances should be considered. If the leader of prayer (rather than an usher) is passing a microphone throughout the congregation during sentence prayers and requests, that leader will be making comments from various places while moving about the room. Even total prostration is prescribed on certain occasions within some Christian traditions. There are various bodily stances that are appropriate to prayer.

But as implied in exercise 10, slouching is excluded. Indeed a prayer leader who slouches may seem to indicate laziness, excessive casualness, disinterest, or even a total lack of respect for what is going on. Equally objectionable are distracting actions on the part of the leader: tugging at the lapels or on a necklace, twisting a lock of hair again and again, or unnecessarily adjusting eyeglasses. Walking around while leading in prayer can also be distracting unless it has a purpose, such as that the leader needs to pass a microphone from worshiper to worshiper.

Unfortunately, many actions that may distract those at prayer are not noticed by the leader due to anxiety or understandable concentration on the task at hand. The leader may need to appoint a friendly critic or two within the congregation who will be bold enough to say, "Do you know that during the prayer you were continuously and rapidly tapping your fingers on the lectern?" (Of course you didn't know it, or you would have stopped. So if no one is willing to tell you, you will annoy the congregation in the same way next week.)

Much of this will seem beside the point if you believe that during prayer all eyes within the congregation will be closed. But certainly they will not be if a printed litany or unison prayer is being used. Nor is it a defensible rule that they should be shut at other times. Particularly during the eucharistic prayer of thanksgiving, for example, all eyes should be open and directed at the Lord's Table where the celebrant stands in the physical stead of Jesus Christ, the host of the banquet.

The popular Protestant direction that prayer be made "with every head bowed and every eye closed" has possibly been more deleterious to Christian praying than any other words regularly uttered in a service of worship. This formula has successfully obscured the fact that prayer can be offered unobtrusively while standing in line at the bank or grocery store, or while waiting at a red traffic light. And many who fail to pray in a restaurant for fear of seeming publicly pious fail to realize a table grace can be said with heads up and eyes open.

When those at prayer keep their eyes open, the matter of the leader's attire also becomes a potential distraction. In many places, vestments are used in an attempt to overcome the visual violence that results from ill-considered combinations of colors, or from plaids, stripes, and polka dots that collide insistently before your eyes. But in recent years, such latitude in the choice of vestments has prevailed as to raise questions about their ability to continue to function in this way. Some contemporary vestments cause as much visual disturbance as the street attire they are intended to hide. Furthermore, even the best of vestments do not conceal some things. A pair of sparkling earrings that dangle wildly with every slight movement of the leader's head or a ring of Super Bowl size on the leader's hand can disrupt the piety of many. Dowdiness and flashiness can be equally distracting. It is not possible, of course, to accommodate one's self to the visual sensibilities of every member of the congregation; still, attire that is modest and neat will be more welcome in most situations than clothing that calls undue attention to itself.

Such considerations may seem to be trifles—things not worthy of discussion in a book on prayer. Shouldn't truly devout people be able to surmount the kinds of distractions being discussed here? Perhaps. But experience reveals it often does not happen according to the ideal situation we have in mind. Therefore all of these "mechanics" related to physical setting and the demeanor of the leader deserve careful consideration in an effort to allow all present to concentrate on prayer without puzzlement, confusion, or distraction. Only in this way can all say the amen with vigor.

Exercise 13

Helping All to Feel Included

Read Ephesians 2:11-22.

As indicated several times previously, it is the goal of the leader to phrase the prayers in such a way that at their close all present can utter a vigorous amen without mental reservations or complaint against the leader. As is often the case in life, attaining the goal is far more difficult than identifying the goal.

In the following prayer text, you will not need to do the usual kind of editing. There will be no occurrences of "Oh God" or "we just come to you asking that you might." Instead, you are to deal entirely with content and are to ask at every point, "Is it possible some persons would feel excluded from this portion of the prayer? If so, why is that the case and what can conceivably be done to invite them more fully into the prayer?" Ponder the passage read from Ephesians, in which the author speaks about the peace that has been made by Christ to bring opposing groups into one and the way in which God has broken down the dividing walls of hostility between persons. As you look at the prayer below, ask where the dividing walls stand and how they can be dismantled so that the congregation can say with one voice, "Amen!" to all that has been presented to God on their behalf.

(Because line-by-line editing is not expected, no space is left between the lines. But line numbers are provided to facilitate the commentary that follows. You may wish to jot notes about your own ideas on a separate sheet of paper, also using the line numbers for reference.)

1   O God our creator, we all praise you for the wonderful week you have given us since last we
2   assembled here to worship you. You are our heavenly Father and have made all men in your
3   image and likeness. We kneel before you in adoration, asking for the grace and power to see
4   your will for our lives. In the light of your holiness, we confess that we are worthless servants
5   who have no right to claim your love. Hear our confession and enable us to be submissive
6   and obedient to your will.

7   All of us hold before you in our hearts those who are ill. Cure them as you cured those
8   upon whom Jesus placed his hands during the days of his ministry. We praise you for the
9   skill and dedication of the medical personnel who attend them and for family members who
10   sacrificially care for them.

11   On this occasion of Mother's Day, we give you thanks for our own mothers and praise you
12   for the opportunity you have given these women to make your creation fruitful. We rejoice in
13   the blessings of the Christian home. We give thanks also for the church, and for the clergy who
14   lead it; enable them to guide our denomination in the ways of goodness and service.

15   We remember also the officials of our city and our nation. Cause them to conserve the
16   precious heritage and holy vision passed on to us by our founders, whose ideals are so
17   threatened now by reckless legislation and disregard for law and order. Remind us that
18   all authorities that exist are instituted by you, and that when we resist them we incur your
19   judgment.

20   Now hear the prayers we utter before your throne of grace, and grant us your shalom through
21   Jesus Christ, who is the only source of salvation.

Commentary

Now we are in the midst of the thorn bush! I have written this prayer in such a way that there is in it something to offend almost everyone. Fortunately not all of those likely to take offense will be in the same congregation on the same day. Nor do I wish to terrify you of giving offense to such an extent that you never dare to open your mouth in public again. Consider this an exercise in what is popularly called "sensitivity training." If you have experienced that kind of heightened awareness, most of what follows will not be new to you. But if you have not, prepare for some challenges.

Lines 1-2. The fact that the leader in prayer has had a wonderful week does not mean that the week has been good for everyone. How can the amen be uttered by the person who has just been diagnosed with a terminal or degenerative disease, or by someone whose child has been arrested for drug possession, or by the person who has filed for bankruptcy? A more inclusive petition could read as follows:

For some of us, this has been a wonderful week. For others it has been a week filled with anxiety, disappointment, or distress. But we have seen your faithfulness in whatever circumstances we find ourselves. Your grace undergirds us in good times and in ill. Continue to assure us of your unfailing love.

Line 2. Here is a double problem with male imagery. Let's deal with the easier issue first. "All men" can be interpreted to mean "all males." Not everyone will so understand it; but increasingly many people will, and they will understandably take offense. "All men" can be changed to "all people," or "all persons." The latter seems to me a little formal, even sociological. Others do not find it to be so. Either option has the effect of bringing into the circle those who otherwise feel excluded.

The more difficult issue has to do with masculine language for God. We need here to elaborate on a matter touched upon in exercise 12. Not only will many worshipers have no objection to calling God "our heavenly Father"; they will indeed be mystified that anyone could object to this biblical title. Objections will tend to come from those who have had a difficult relationship with their earthly fathers and therefore cannot understand the "fatherhood" of God to be anything but threatening. More basic objections will be raised by those who understand that the language we use not only reflects our understanding of reality but actually shapes it. If God is always spoken of as a male, we become blinded to characteristics of God that are expressed in female imagery, and for these there is ample precedent in Scripture. Various approaches to dealing with exclusively masculine language for God are possible, including (1) expanded language: "our heavenly Father and Mother"; (2) alternative language that is roughly equivalent: "our heavenly Parent"; (3) substitute language: "our Creator" or "our Maker" or "our Guardian and Guide." In order to deal with this issue you will need to understand both your congregation and your denomination. What is acceptable will vary greatly from place to place. What one group of worshipers regards as appropriate inclusivity, another group may experience as shocking and outrageous. The former can say the amen heartily, the latter not at all.

Lines 4-6. Historically Christians have been quite content to be considered worthless servants who have no claim upon God's love. The words of Jesus in Luke 17:10 can be called upon in evidence here, as can historic prayers in which we confess ourselves to be "miserable sinners," people "provoking most justly thy wrath and indignation against us." But recently we have come to learn much about the consequences of low self-esteem. Some Christians, even while granting that we are indeed sinful, question the appropriateness of saying that we are worthless or miserable. Similarly, obedience to God can be considered a virtue; but particularly when affixed to the term "submissive," the language again can seem unduly harsh to the contemporary ear. Too often males have abused females, wrongly using as justification biblical language about the need for wives to be submissive to their husbands. Christian worship dare not jettison confession, however much the prevailing culture may wish it otherwise. But alternative biblical language that is not damaging or offensive can be chosen, such as:

In the light of your holiness, we confess our imperfections and our willful rebellion against your ways. By your love, which redeemed us on the cross, make us conformable to your will; enable us to walk in your paths as joyful daughters and sons who are saved by grace, not as tortured underlings who quake in fear before you.

Lines 7-8. Although it may seem to some like hair-splitting, it is often pointed out that frequently God heals the sick but does not cure them: that is, the physical difficulty may not disappear, and indeed may lead directly to death. Still, God heals the sufferer of undue anxiety or of a wholly negative attitude toward sickness and death; or God enables reconciliation to occur between persons who may have had a severely strained relationship previously. In this sense, approaching permanent disability or death without fear can be seen as a form of "healing." Death itself can be viewed as the ultimate healing; though a "cure" in the medical sense does not occur to the physical body, the believer is received into the realm of life eternal.

Lines 8-10. This sentence would seem utterly inoffensive were it not for an experience I had when conducting a worship service in New Zealand. I knew that this Sunday evening service frequently was attended by persons employed at a hospital across the street. At the close of the service, someone in a nurse's uniform approached me; with faltering voice and tearful eyes she said: "I am so upset about not being included in your prayers for those who work at the hospital." I had no idea what to make of her comment and so said in response: "But I specifically asked God's blessing upon all medical personnel. I did not want to enumerate individual groups such as physicians, lab technicians, nurses, custodial staff, and the like, for fear of omitting some crucial category." At this point the woman began to sob and said, "But that is just the problem. Nurses are not medical personnel. So you left us out." By then I was utterly befuddled to the point of questioning this person's mental balance. But she recited an account later corroborated by others, as follows. Not too long before, a medical insurer refused to pay claims for nursing care because their policies covered only payment to "medical personnel," from which category nurses were intended to be excluded. Strangely (to my way of thinking, at least), the court ruled in favor of the insurance company and declared that nurses were indeed not to be considered medical personnel. I recount all of this to make a point: "You can't win 'em all." Sometimes our attempts to include everyone backfire on us because we do not understand the local use of language, even when it is our native tongue. I had given the prayer from notes, not a complete manuscript. I suppose I should have written it out in full and had a citizen of New Zealand read the text of my prayer in advance, but the need for this did not even occur to me. I hope the nurse took some comfort from my profound apology and made some allowance for ignorance across national boundaries.

Lines 11-12. Here the excluded may number legion. It is obvious that all fathers are excluded. (Yes, there is a Father's Day a month or so later, but it rarely receives anything like the hoopla that accompanies Mother's Day.) How does a person who has had a very injurious relationship with his or her mother respond to this prayer? What feeling does this prayer evoke from those who have never had an opportunity to become mothers, though they may have wanted to do so very earnestly? Does the phrase "make your creation fruitful" mean that those who may have consciously chosen not to bear children are somehow anti-creation? Does it imply that the more children one has had, the more one has honored God? If so, what do we say about the danger of overpopulation on our planet? The prayer might better say something like this:

On the day on which our society honors mothers, we give thanks for all persons who have nurtured the young, whether as parents or guardians or caregivers. We remember not only those who have lovingly reared their own children but those who have taken into their hearts the orphaned, the abused, the unwanted children of our world and have shown them love, even as you show love for us. Comfort those for whom this is a difficult day due to sorrow or regret or deep alienation.

Lines 12-13. Imagine in the congregation a devout Christian woman who has established a home with an equally devout Jew (or Muslim, or adherent of some other religion). Does she feel included when only "the Christian home" is mentioned as a cause for rejoicing? Alternatively consider this:

We rejoice in the homes of all who strive to understand you and diligently seek to serve you and the world you offer to us as a gift. Show yourself to them more fully day by day and strengthen them in faith.

Lines 13-14. Are all of the leaders of the church ordained? Is only one denomination to be the subject of our intercessions? A more inclusive alternative:

We give you thanks also for the church and for all who lead it, both lay and clergy, within our denomination and within all other communities of Christian faith. Enable them to guide your people in the ways of goodness and service.

Lines 15-17. Taken as a whole, these lines seem to have a clear political agenda. All of the founders apparently were saints, and their modern-day counterparts (or at least some of them) are gross sinners bent on lawlessness and anarchy. And is it possible to get beyond the boundaries of our own city and country? Here is another possible approach:

We remember those who bear the responsibility of public office, in our own city and nation, and across the world. Place within each of them a commitment to justice and a passion for the welfare of all, particularly of those unable to speak up for their own causes. Enable all leaders to set aside that which benefits them and their friends alone, and to embrace the fullest good we can envision.

Lines 17-19. Here is a curious juxtaposition, probably engendered by the desire to provide a biblical "proof-text" for the viewpoint of the leader in prayer. What is the difficulty? Line 17 alleges that the country is being run by legislators who are reckless and other leaders who care nothing for civic order. But line 18 suggests that we are to knuckle under to these scoundrels because God has put them in office! To do otherwise may incur divine displeasure on a grand scale. This strange, self-contradictory theology of political order springs from an allusion to Romans 13:1-2, apparently inserted as a point of argument. This is a good illustration concerning why difficult biblical passages are to be used as the basis of sermons, carefully thought out and constructed, not as sentences to be casually dropped into prayers. In this prayer, lines 17-19 would best be omitted.

Line 20. Only if a congregation has had extensive exposure both to the word "shalom" and to the breadth of its meaning in the Hebrew Bible should such a term be inserted into prayer. Even then, what understanding will be brought to this petition by visitors to the congregation on that day? Likely they will pause to puzzle over the strange word and perhaps will suppose they have misheard it; then they may try to discover what word they were intended to hear instead. Thereby, they will become lost to the point of dropping out of the prayer. In a sermon, a reference may well be made to *shalom*, followed by a goodly explanation; but the rhetoric of prayer and that of preaching should not be confused.

Line 21. Whether this line presents a problem depends on one's interpretation of "the only source of salvation." Is this to be taken to mean that anyone who is not explicitly a Christian believer is damned? If so, those who understand the grace of God more broadly may feel excluded. Or is the phrase to be understood to mean that the grace of Christ reaches beyond the confines of the Christian church and that when persons of other faiths find hope in God, they discover this through the same divine graciousness we identify with Jesus? If so, worshipers who are terrified of anything that seems to smack of universal salvation will feel excluded. Interpretations of such language vary from denomination to denomination, and even to a great extent within the same denomination. Once again, it is necessary that the leader know the basic system of belief out of which the congregation is operating.

As I noted at the beginning of the commentary on this section, it is not my intention to terrify you to the point that you wish never to have to pray in public again. But it is to alert you to the complexity of human language with both its possibilities and its limitations. The discipline of thought and language needed to invite all into the household of God is worth every effort we can put into it.

I have rewritten this prayer to such an extent that it did not seem helpful to show my editing by way of interlining the original text in the way to which you have become accustomed. So it may be useful here to see the revision as a whole.

O God, our Creator:
  For some of us, this has been a wonderful week.
  For others it has been a week filled with anxiety, disappointment, or distress.
But we have seen your faithfulness in whatever circumstances we find ourselves.
Your grace undergirds us in good times and in ill.
Continue to assure us of your unfailing love.
In the light of your holiness,
  we confess our imperfections
  and our willful rebellion against your ways.

By your love, which redeemed us on the cross,
 make us conformable to your will;
enable us to walk in your paths
 as joyful daughters and sons who are saved by grace,
 not as tortured underlings who quake in fear before you.

All of us hold before you in our hearts those who are ill.
Minister to them according to your wisdom,
 even as Jesus did in the days of his ministry among us,
 that they may know of your constant care and compassion.
We praise you for those who attend them in hospitals
 and other centers of healing;
 for family members,
 and for all who sacrificially care for them.

On the day on which our society honors mothers,
 we give thanks for all persons who have nurtured the young,
 whether as parents or guardians or caregivers.
We remember not only those who have lovingly reared their own children
but those who have taken into their hearts
 the orphaned,
 the abused,
 the unwanted children of our world
 and have shown them love, even as you show love for us.
Comfort those for whom this is a difficult day due to
 sorrow or regret or deep alienation.
We rejoice in the homes of all who strive to understand you
 and diligently seek to serve you
 and the world you offer to us as a gift.
Show yourself to them more fully day by day,
 and strengthen them in faith.
We give you thanks also for the church,
 and for all who lead it, both lay and clergy,
 within our denomination
 and within all other communities of Christian faith.
Enable them to guide your people in the ways of goodness and service.

We remember those who bear the responsibility of public office,
 in our own city and nation,
 and across the world.
Place within each of them
 a commitment to justice
 and a passion for the welfare of all,
 particularly of those unable to speak up for their own causes.
Enable all leaders to set aside
 that which benefits them and their friends alone,
 and to embrace the fullest good we can envision.
Now accept the prayers we utter
 before your throne of grace;
and grant us your abiding peace through Jesus Christ our Savior.

Helping all to feel included is necessary but not easy. Particularly when racial and cultural differences characterize the members of the worshiping assembly, it may be difficult to know what causes feelings of exclusion by some groups, let alone how to prevent such feelings. Help concerning some of these differences can be found in *Worship Across Cultures: A Handbook* by Kathy Black.[12] This work outlines various practices of worship in a way you may find useful; although written specifically with reference to The United Methodist Church, much of the information will apply to other denominations also.

Exercise 14

The Lost Art of Lament

Read Lamentations 1:12-16.

It is a strange thing to observe that Christians at public prayer so infrequently engage in lament despite the fact that the Bible contains a book called Lamentations. That book is very brief, by its size perhaps concealing how widespread lament is in the canon as a whole. The Psalms are full of laments, as is Job. Jesus weeps over the city of Jerusalem and utters a loud cry of anguish from the cross. The final book of the New Testament contains poignant cries of distress by the saints who are suffering persecution.

Probably most Christians do much more lamenting over the back fence than in the house of the Lord. We engage in "ain't it a shame" discussions with friends and neighbors far more regularly than we cry out in distress to God. To be blunt: Lamentation has gotten a bad name in the church. People who complain are looked upon as lacking in faith. One is supposed to trust God in every circumstance without complaint. The silver lining of every cloud is to be identified at once, no matter how tragic the circumstances. In preparing this exercise, I happened to look at a section of an NRSV study Bible that contains some eight hundred entries in its dictionary of biblical terms. *Lament* and *lamentation* are not to be found there. How revealing of the blind spot that afflicts us!

Hence in the church we hardly know what to do when our town has experienced racial tension or gun violence in the schools, when our family has lost a member through suicide or an avoidable accident, when the nation faces an international crisis or loses a leader to an assassin's bullet. Our inability to express our raw pain in such instances is palpable. We smile stoically, sing "Amazing Grace," and mutter nonsense about God having done these things for some good reason. (Do we really believe that the God made known in Jesus Christ engineers shooting sprees by students, reigns of terror by dictators, and accidents that occur when drivers are under the influence of alcohol or other drugs?) Those who suffer the greatest pain thereby feel excluded. They dare not admit their deepest feelings, and the church gives them no liturgical outlet for their distress. The lack of habits of lamentation in our time constitutes an enormous but generally unrecognized form of exclusion.

Far better that we should do what biblical people did all the time: Allow people—indeed encourage people—to cry out in agony to the God who, far from causing us pain, suffers with us under it. Lament can be justified on practical grounds—it is cathartic, enabling us to feel better because we have gotten something "off our chests." That is not an unimportant reason for lament, but there is a far better one. Good lamentation is honesty before the God who already knows how we feel. Read Psalm 139:1-6 for amplification. To put on a smiley face before the All-Knowing One is to engage in deceit. Furthermore, God is both willing and able to accept whatever venom we spew out. Not only to accept it, but to redeem it, to transform it.

Therein lies the key to understanding what for many Christians is the most troubling passage in the Bible with which they are familiar—Psalm 137. It begins so beautifully:

By the rivers of Babylon—
　　there we sat down and there we wept
　　when we remembered Zion.
On the willows there
　　we hung up our harps.
For there our captors
　　asked us for songs,

and our tormentors asked for mirth, saying,
   "Sing us one of the songs of Zion!"
How could we sing the LORD's song
   in a foreign land?

If I forget you, O Jerusalem,
   let my right hand wither!
Let my tongue cling to the roof of my mouth,
if I do not remember you,
if I do not set Jerusalem
   above my highest joy.

Then comes the shocking conclusion:

Remember, O LORD, against the Edomites
   the day of Jerusalem's fall,
      how they said, "Tear it down! Tear it down!
Down to its foundations!"
O daughter Babylon, you devastator!
Happy shall they be who pay you back
   what you have done to us!
Happy shall they be who take your little ones
   and dash them against the rock!

Is Scripture telling us that God wants the babies of our enemies to be dashed against the stones? Not likely! The message is rather this: When we yearn for revenge, God knows that. Better we should turn our vengeful desires over to the only One who can correctly judge the situation than that we should take things into our own hands—and in the process try to conceal what God already knows full well about us. By including this Psalm and many other passages akin to it, the Scriptures are commending honest confession, not retributive violence.

Often biblical complaint is sandwiched between statements of trust. The prayer begins with some word of confidence that God will answer the sufferer; then follows the anguish. Finally there is a resolution that reveals hope and peace. Psalms 55–59 follow this pattern. But sometimes the pain is so intense that the lament begins in anguish with no indication that God may show favor. See Psalms 22 and 60 as examples, and note the final bursts of confidence in each instance. As we have seen in Psalm 137, sometimes there is no resolution even at the close of the lament. The forms vary, but always there is candor.

Here is a form of lament such as could be appropriate in a community after some violent form of activity that has resulted in death and terror. Such a prayer might have been included in a prayer service held immediately after the bombing of an office building in Oklahoma or the shootings in a school in Colorado.

O God, you are our help and strength,	Psalm 124:8
* our refuge in the time of trouble.*	Psalm 37:39
In you our ancestors trusted;	
They trusted and you delivered them.	Psalm 22:4
When we do not know how to pray as we ought,	
* your very Spirit intercedes for us*	
* with sighs too deep for words.*	Romans 8:26
We plead for the intercession now, Gracious One.	
For desolation and destruction are in our streets,	Isaiah 59:7
* and terror dances before us.*	Job 41:22
Our hearts faint; our knees tremble;	
* our bodies quake; all faces grow pale.*	Nahum 2:10
Our eyes are spent from weeping	
* and our stomachs churn.*	Lamentations 2:11

How long, O Lord, how long	Isaiah 6:11
must we endure this devastation?	
How long will destruction lay waste at noonday?	Psalm 91:6
Why does violence flourish	
while peace is taken prisoner?	
Rouse yourself! Do not cast us off in times of trouble.	Psalm 44:23
Come to our help;	
redeem us for the sake of your steadfast love.	Psalm 44:26
For you are a gracious God	
abounding in steadfast love and faithfulness.	Exodus 34:6
By the power of the cross,	1 Corinthians 1:17
through which you redeemed the world,	
bring to an end hostility	Ephesians 2:14
and establish justice in the gate.	Amos 5:15
For you will gather together your people into that place	
where mourning and crying and pain	
will be no more,	
and tears will be wiped from every eye.	Revelation 21:4
Hasten the day, O God of our salvation.	
Accomplish it quickly!	Isaiah 60:22

This prayer consists of three elements: appeals to God to act, complaint, and words of trust. It could well include intercessions for those who are suffering most directly, but these might equally well come in some other portion of the service for this occasion. The prayer could also deal with matters of guilt and judgment. These could be set into this prayer something like this:

Save us from the smug condemnation of the guilty.	
For we do not understand our own actions,	
much less theirs.	
The good we ourselves wish to do,	
everyone of us fails to do.	
And we submit to the very sins we hate.	Romans 7:15
Have mercy on us all.	

But if this prayer is to be offered immediately after the tragic event has occurred, it may be too soon for such a petition. Another day may be more suitable. Or, as in the case of possible intercessions, these needs may be dealt with in other parts of the day's liturgy. The force of the lament can be blunted by trying to heap too many different kinds of things into its form.

Now I want you to try your hand at writing two differing forms of lament. First consider the situation of an individual who is undergoing difficult times due to the betrayal of someone very close: close friend, family member, professional colleague, and so on. Identify the situation. Next see if any parallel situation has existed in your life that helps you better to understand the anger and frustration of the person offended. Then write your lament, relying on Psalm 55 for inspiration. You will not need to use everything in the Psalm. What you do use may fall in a different order, and you may also draw on other passages of Scripture as you wish.

Although the lament will contain intimations of trust in God, do not attempt to gloss over the rage and anguish the sufferer feels on the theory that Christians are to be forgiving; for true forgiveness may not be possible until first we have confronted ourselves honestly and opened our anguished hearts to God.

Individual Lament in the Time of Betrayal

_____
_____
_____
_____
_____
_____
_____
_____
_____
_____
_____
_____
_____
_____
_____
_____
_____
_____
_____
_____
_____
_____
_____
_____
_____

Do not proceed until you have finished writing your lament.

Now look closely at what you have done. Read it aloud. Does it sound like honest lamentation, or is it too "tame" to be candid? To what extent does your prayer share in the spirit of the Psalm?

Below is my own version of a lamentation related to Psalm 55. I have envisioned a business owner whose partner has unexpectedly left the firm to start a competing business and has taken along all mailing lists of clients, the secrets of the success of the operation, and has recruited many current employees to work for the new firm.

An Individual Lament in the Time of Betrayal

Based on Psalm 55.

Receive my prayer, O God,
and do not hide yourself from my anguish.
Answer me, for I am troubled and distraught.
Terrors have fallen upon me,
and trembling comes over me.
I do not know if I can endure.

For the one I trusted has violated a covenant with me
with speech smoother than butter
and words softer than oil,
taking in those who worked beside me
and making them my enemies.

It is not my old competitors who taunt me—
I could bear that.
It is not adversaries who deal insolently with me,
but those whom I trusted,
those with whom I have shared happy times.
It is my equals, my companions, my friends
who have risen up against me.
For envy and greed have become their friends.
Evening and morning and at noon
I utter my complaint and moan.
For what shall become of me?
Horror overwhelms me.

Let disaster come upon them, O God.
Confound their plans and humble them.
Send them down to defeat.
Devour their dreams of prosperity
and cause them to have the fear that I feel.
Deliver me from disaster and despair,
and do not let me be put to shame.

For in you do I trust,
and you will save me.
Accept me for the sake of Jesus Christ,
and sustain me with your goodness.

Now write a corporate lament, suitable for use in a congregational service of worship. Begin by identifying the kind of occasion in the community. For example, a trusted community leader has been caught embezzling funds; or, a hate group has killed a member of a minority group; or a halfway house for trouble youths has been torched, apparently by neighbors who publicly said, "We don't want that kind of thing in our neighborhood." Use Psalms 17 and 27 as sources, but write the prayer in the plural ("we, us, our, ours").

A Corporate Lament in the Time of Anguish

_____
_____
_____
_____
_____
_____
_____
_____
_____
_____
_____
_____
_____
_____
_____
_____
_____
_____
_____
_____
_____
_____
_____
_____
_____
_____
_____
_____
_____
_____
_____

When you have finished, read your lament aloud. Is it authentic to the situation you had in mind when you began? How can it be improved? Edit it further as you deem necessary.

Exercise 15

The Pastoral Prayer and Related Forms

Read John 17.

Y ou have heard perhaps of this formula concerning what a comprehensive prayer should contain:

Adoration
Confession
Thanksgiving
Supplication

The first letters when read top to bottom form the word *acts*, as a way of enabling you to recall the formula. If this memory device aids you, fine. But please note two things: (1) its stated purpose and (2) what it does not include.

(1) The purpose of the memory device is to enable you to construct a comprehensive prayer. Often such a prayer is intended for a service in which there is to be only one prayer on that day. Hence this prayer has to include everything: praise of God, confession of sin, thanksgiving to God, and requests—also known as supplications or, alternatively, as petitions.

Just to confuse you, some books on prayer make a distinction between two kinds of requests:

Requests for others = Intercession
Requests for ourselves = Supplication

But usually "supplication" is a generic term that covers requests of both sorts.

Back to the main topic. Particularly in certain churches that grew out of the Puritan tradition, one prayer was used within most services. Since usually it was the pastor who prepared and led the prayer, it came to be known as the "pastoral prayer." (Note carefully the spelling. Often the term appears in print incorrectly as the "pastorial" prayer, and then the nonexistent *i* creates a mispronunciation—a four-syllable word rather than a three-syllable word.)

If you are in fact a pastor, note carefully that the pastoral prayer is a prayer you utter in public *in the name of* the congregation. It is not your *personal prayer for* the congregation, which you utter day by day in your private prayer closet. Your personal prayer will contain the names of individuals and matters that you are expected to hold in secrecy. Confidential matters must not be aired in the pastoral prayer, nor should names be included without the permission of the persons involved. To disregard this advice is to breach the pastor-parishioner bond of trust.

If you are not a pastor, there are times when a comprehensive prayer is appropriate, whatever title may be given to it. In addition to adoration, confession, thanksgiving, and supplication, the prayer may include lament. And these elements do not have to fall in the same order each time. Thanksgiving may well be combined with adoration, for example; or, thanksgiving may be reserved until the end of the prayer so that our praying closes on a joyous note of gratitude. If lament is included, this may well either precede or follow confession; for in many instances what we lament is closely related to our sins, particularly the sin of not trusting the goodness and mercy of God.

In the past, comprehensive prayers could be seemingly interminable—twenty minutes long, for example, in a time when sermons went on for two hours or more. Hence such a prayer came to be known as "the long prayer." (I will leave it to you to judge whether that designation was intended as an insult or simply as an honest description.) Today in most circles a prayer even of ten or fifteen minutes' duration will likely be regarded as excessively long.

In many services the comprehensive prayer is not needed; for much of the work it does is done by shorter prayers throughout the service. Most services now begin with some type of prayer of adoration, either before or after an opening hymn of praise. Either shortly thereafter or much further along in the service (after the sermon, for example), a prayer of confession will be used. An extended prayer of thanksgiving precedes the distribution of the bread and cup if the Lord's Supper is celebrated; if the Eucharist is not observed, there may be a briefer act of thanksgiving following the offering or at some other point. In such a context, a comprehensive prayer is redundant; therefore the service likely will include instead a time of petition, known variously as "the prayers of the people," "the prayer of the faithful," "the intercessions," "the biddings," or "the concerns" (see exercise 20).

When a single comprehensive prayer is in order, any single category covered elsewhere on that day may be omitted. Not only is there no reason, for example, to confess twice; but doing so may seem to suggest that we did not believe the promises or declarations of forgiveness that followed the first prayer of confession for that day.

(2) Notice what the A-C-T-S formula excludes. Although the comprehensive prayer can be something of a catchall, there is one thing it should not contain (nor should any other prayer) and that is information. God does not need to be informed; therefore bits of information included actually are announcements to the congregation under the guise of prayer. For example: It is reported that the president of a church-related school neglected to make a pertinent announcement in the required chapel service at the beginning of a class day. Realizing the omission, he included this in his closing prayer: "And we ask you, O God, to look in your mercy upon Prof. Jones, who is ill with the flu this morning and whose classes therefore will not meet today or possibly tomorrow as well." I cannot attest to the truth of that tale; it may be apocryphal. But I can swear on a stack of Bibles that I once heard the following. "And God, we ask you to watch over John Doe, a member of our congregation, who was injured in an auto accident at 2:00 P.M. yesterday on route 15, and is now in stable condition in room 304 of Memorial Hospital." God does not need this information. If its inclusion in prayer is not technically a way of reinforcing "the absent deity syndrome," certainly its inclusion implies that God is more unknowing than any Christian heresy has ever suggested.

Try now editing a comprehensive prayer:

1   Gracious are you, O God, and worthy of our praise and service. We know that you

2   have redeemed us and that you have called us by name. And Lord, we realize that the whole

3   creation is filled with thy glory. Blessed art thou for ever and ever.

4   But in the light of your perfection we confess that we see our own failings. We confess

5   that we have been preoccupied by our own needs. We confess that we have neglected our

6   families and that we have ignored others. We confess that we not been generous with our

7   time and money. Forgive us, we pray.

8   We just want to give thanks to you for your goodness to us in spite of our sin. And

9   we want to thank you for the many gifts you have given to us that we enjoy. Lord, we bless you

10   for the opportunities and challenges you set before us, as well as your gifts. We are among

11   the most fortunate people in the world. Our standard of living is the envy of people all over.

12   We work hard and are diligent in all that we do.

13   We pray for those who mourn the deaths of others. Comfort them, we pray. We also

14   pray for those who are sick, that they may be healed by God. May we do what we can to help

15   them in the time of need. Be with the president of the United States and the Congress.

16   Direct the way they govern us, O God. Also help the leaders of the world. Many of them

17   need to work more diligently to improve the lives of their people. People of great faith and

18   hope founded our church nearly two hundred years ago. Their successors made great

19   sacrifices to enable us to be here today. So, God, be with all current leaders of our church and

20   keep their eyes on the mission you have given us.

21   These things we ask through Christ our Savior.

Do not proceed to the next page until you have completed your editing of this prayer.

Suggested Revisions and Commentary

1   Gracious are you, O God, and worthy of our praise and service. ~~We know that you~~

      You

2   have redeemed us and ~~that you have~~ called us by name. ~~And Lord, we realize that the~~ whole

      The

3   creation is filled with ~~thy~~ glory. Blessed ~~art thou~~ for ever and ever.

      your   are you

4   ~~But in~~ the light of your perfection ~~we confess that~~ we see our own failings. We confess

      In

5   that we have been preoccupied by our own needs. ~~We confess that we have neglected our~~

      Forgive us for times when we have

6   ~~families and that we have ignored others. We confess that we not been generous with our~~

      neglected others and have lacked generosity. By your power, restore us to faithfulness.

7   ~~time and money. Forgive us, we pray.~~

      Cause your Spirit to breathe into us new life, that we may show forth your glory.

8   We ~~just want to~~ give thanks ~~to you~~ for your goodness to us in spite of our sin. ~~And~~

9   ~~we want to thank~~ you for ~~the many gifts you have given to us that we enjoy. Lord, we bless you~~

      We bless   your many gifts and also

10 for the opportunities and challenges you set before ~~us, as well as your gifts. We are among~~

      us.

11 ~~the most fortunate people in the world. Our standard of living is the envy of people all over.~~

12 ~~We work hard and are diligent in all that we do.~~

13 ~~We pray for~~ those who mourn ~~the deaths of others. Comfort them, we pray. We also~~

      Comfort

Heal the sick, that they may serve you with joy. Make known to us how best we may minister
14 ~~pray for those who are sick, that they may be healed by God. May we do what we can to help~~

to them and with them.　　Direct　　　　　　　　　　　　　States, the Congress, and the
15 ~~them in the time of need. Be with~~ the president of the United ~~States and the Congress.~~

Supreme Court, that they may govern wisely. Motivate　　　　　　　　　to work
16 ~~Direct the way they govern us, O God. Also help~~ the leaders of the world. ~~Many of them~~

　　　　　　　　　　　　　　　　　　all
17 ~~need to work more~~ diligently to improve the lives of ~~their~~ people. ~~People of great faith and~~

18 ~~hope founded our church nearly two hundred years ago. Their successors made great~~

　　　　　　　　　　　　　　　　　　　　　　　Enable the
19 ~~sacrifices to enable us to be here today. So, God, be with all current~~ leaders of our church ~~and~~

to be faithful to your mission, that we may thereby honor our founders and those after them,
20 ~~keep their eyes on the mission you have given us.~~

21 whose sacrifices made possible our own ministry. These things we ask through Christ our Savior.

As pastoral prayers go, this is brief, particularly in its edited form. It does, however, follow the ACTS pattern, with one paragraph being devoted to each component.

Lines 1-3 are edited to delete words that do no work, and to impose a uniformity of style (in relation to occasional lapses into archaic English forms).

The original **lines 4-7** contain statements to which many worshipers may not be able to say amen. Some persons may have neglected others and been ungenerous; but other worshipers cannot identify with these particular sins. So the confessions have been recast. The original lines were confession only; always after an admission of sin it is well to ask God not merely to forgive us but also to transform us and to keep us faithful.

Lines 8-10 are reduced in bulk in the edited version.

Lines 10-12 constitute information (or opinions, at least) and are inappropriately self-congratulatory. I prefer to delete them. But they could also be recast into petitions, as follows:

> *Enable us, as a people of great material affluence, to share with others, to*
> *bear the burdens of others, and to work diligently for the benefit of all.*

Were this done, however, the paragraph would consist of supplication as well as thanksgiving.

Lines 13-15a are edited to strengthen their expression and flow; a purpose is added to the petition for healing in line 14. The words "and with them" in line 15 are intended to alleviate the notion that the sick have no ministry of their own, but that we must do everything for them.

In **lines 15-16**, the Supreme Court is added to represent before God the full complement of national governmental branches in the United States. Readers in other nations will need to make adaptations according to the varying forms of government (for example, monarch, parliament, and high court). Where the pastoral prayer is used with some regularity, care should be taken that frequent mention is also made of regional and local governmental authorities.

Lines 16-17 in their original form are inappropriately judgmental; particularly offensive is the petition that others may work *more* diligently, in contrast to the assertion in line 12 that "we . . . are diligent in all that we do."

Lines 17-20 begin with a great deal of information. The edited version places much of that into a clause of purpose. Over time church leaders of various ranks (bishops, deacons, lay leaders, presbyters, teachers, and so on) should be prayed for as should the church at local, national, and international levels. When denominational conventions and conferences are being held, these also are appropriate concerns for public prayer by the congregation.

Praying About Controversial Issues

Read 1 Corinthians 13.

If the whole church is to say amen, great care must be taken when dealing with controversial issues. On the Sunday prior to an election, it will not do to ask God that one particular candidate or party may trounce the others at the polls. It is highly unlikely that everyone in a congregation holds the same political opinions, and taking sides so evidently immediately will alienate those of opposing views.

A fundamental principle in dealing with controversy is to discover what kinds of things can be agreed upon. Before an election, surely everyone can agree that citizenship implies the duty to participate in the electoral process, that citizens should be as informed as possible about the issues before them, and that the ideal outcome of the election will benefit the general welfare of the nation and the world. Therefore it is appropriate to pray that citizens may accept their responsibility to vote, that they may approach their task with preparation and may be given wisdom in their choices, and that the welfare of all may be benefited.

When trying to be evenhanded, it is necessary to avoid terms that may seem "loaded," whether they are intended to be so by the leader of prayer or not. Obviously the names of parties or their candidates are not to be dropped into public intercessions. Short of that, there are other ways of seeming to take sides in an election. Suppose, for example, that the prayer includes this petition: "Enable us to maintain a democracy in which free choice is enjoyed by all." Seems innocuous enough, doesn't it? But not if a hot-button issue in that campaign has been abortion, and those in favor of abortion rights have widely used the slogan "Free Choice." As a leader of prayer, you may have used the term "free choice" very generically and with no intention of addressing the abortion debate in any way. But that is not how some in the congregation will hear what you have said. So it is necessary to know what the loaded terms are and how to avoid them.

To broaden the discussion of terms beyond the political sphere: In my own denomination at the moment, there is a great division of opinion about the nature of homosexuality and whether or not homosexual orientation can be reversed. Those who believe it can be altered sometimes designate themselves as being part of a "transforming congregation"—by the power of God, they believe, homosexual persons can be transformed into heterosexuals. Those who believe otherwise may designate themselves "reconciling congregations"; they believe that, in most cases at least, such orientation cannot be changed and therefore reconciliation needs to occur between those of differing sexual dispositions.

As Christians, it is very difficult to be against either transformation or reconciliation; both concepts are deeply rooted in the gospel, and the New Testament uses both terms freely. But within the church context just described, the use of these terms becomes very tricky. If the leader asks God to "make us a transforming community," that may not be heard as a general statement derived from New Testament vocabulary but as a speech in favor of one side of the sexual orientation debate. Even to alter the terms slightly and to request that God make "our congregation a people who bring about reconciliation" may readily be interpreted as a speech on the other side of the debate. The problem with this particular language interpretation did not exist twenty-five years ago, and even today is limited to certain denominations. Therefore sensitivity to what language connotes in a particular time and setting is essential. (Recall my experience about praying for "medical personnel" while in New Zealand?)

For that reason, I urgently suggest that when you are to deal with controversial issues in prayer, you write the prayer out, even if you pray without written preparation in every other case. I do not have great confidence in the human ability to steer clear of all loaded terms when praying without such preparation. Controversial issues should not be avoided while at prayer, although prayer needs to be one part of a comprehensive program of study and discussion done in a variety of settings. Bible studies, forums for the open discussion of issues of ethics, sermons, and presentations by knowledgeable persons all are useful in addition to prayer. Choosing the proper venue for addressing differing aspects of a controversial issue is as important as the choice of language used when at prayer.

Now try your hand at editing a prayer for use in the following situation: A referendum is being held on increasing property taxes to enhance public education in your community. The populace seems to be about evenly divided, with the pro-tax people asserting that "Property ownership implies public responsibility," while the anti-tax people reply that "Those who benefit should be those who pay." The latter side believes that property owners without children to be educated in the public school system should not have to bear tax increases, and that therefore some other means of raising revenue needs to be devised. This is a prayer for use in a service of worship two days prior to the vote.

1   Oh God, our Source and Sovereign, to you we come with our confusion and divergent

2   views on the matter before us this week. We just want to ask you to show us how best we may

3   contribute to the responsibility we have for educating thy children in this community. O God,

4   let us put aside selfish motives that cause us to consider our own pocketbooks ahead of

5   the public good. May we accept willingly whatever sacrifices we need to make as persons

6   of privilege in order to work for the benefit of everyone, not just the benefit of some of us,

7   O Lord. We just thank you for the teachers and administrators of our schools and for the

8   generations before them who have prepared the way and provided for our community a

9   fine educational system, which must be preserved if we are to continue to be an educated

10   populace in a democracy that treats all equally, so we can dwell in peace and prosperity

11   as one nation under God. Lord Jesus, in your ministry on earth you taught everyone who

12   would listen. May we continue your ministry of teaching in your name and may all who

13   learn submit themselves to your will and your way. In Jesus name we pray.

Do not proceed to the next page until you have completed your editing of the above prayer.

Suggested Revisions and Commentary

The suggested revisions of this prayer are given in two parts. (1) Immediately below are preliminary revisions that have to do primarily with structure and style. (2) Then follow comments on basic content, with a complete reconstruction of the prayer provided.

       O

1   ~~Oh~~ God, our Source and Sovereign, to you we come with our confusion and divergent

                                  Show

2   views on the matter before us this week. ~~We just want to ask you to show~~ us how best we may

                           your

3   contribute to the responsibility we have for educating ~~thy~~ children in this community. ~~O God,~~

   Help us to

4   ~~let us~~ put aside selfish motives that cause us to consider our own pocketbooks ahead of

          Give us the courage to

5   the public good. ~~May we~~ accept willingly whatever sacrifices we need to make as persons

                                 us.

6   of privilege in order to work for the benefit of everyone, not just the benefit of some of ~~us,~~

          Thank

7   ~~O Lord. We just thank~~ you for the teachers and administrators of our schools and for the

8   generations before them who have prepared the way and provided for our community a

         system. Enable us to preserve it, that we may

9   fine educational ~~system, which must be preserved if we are to~~ continue to be an educated

10 populace in a democracy that treats all equally, so we can dwell in peace and prosperity

              you. For through the ministry of Jesus

11 as one nation under ~~God. Lord Jesus, in your ministry on earth~~ you taught everyone who

         Guide us as we seek to   teaching, that all who learn may

12 would listen. ~~May we~~ continue your ministry of ~~teaching in your name and may all who~~

                          Jesus'

13 ~~learn~~ submit themselves to your will and your way. In ~~Jesus~~ name we pray.

This preliminary editing does not yet produce an acceptable prayer; for basic issues can be addressed only through a major reconstruction of the prayer. Reasons for most of the editorial changes should be evident; you can see that this exercise is a review of a number of principles previously discussed.

Particularly note, however, the trinitarian confusion introduced at line 11. The prayer is addressed to God, but at line 11 Jesus is addressed. Neither the Father nor the Spirit is similarly addressed, and so it would appear that God exists in only one Person. In the closing, Jesus (to whom we have been speaking directly) is mentioned indirectly ("in Jesus' name we pray"), creating yet more confusion. Hence the changes in lines 11-13.

Also in line 11 note that "in Jesus name" correctly appears as "in Jesus' name." This implies more than the use of an apostrophe. It has also to do with pronunciation. The possessive of *Jesus* is *Jesus'* not *Jesus's*. The written form dictates the spoken form. To the ear, the correct possessive form—*Jesus'*—sounds exactly like the proper name *without* a possessive added. The possessive is not pronounced *Jesuses*. The rule is as follows: If adding an *s* sound to form a possessive creates three sibilant sounds (that is, hissing noises) in rapid succession, do not add the possessive *s*. The reason for this odd rule is to save the ear from having to endure a sentence that sounds this way: "For conscience-s sake, Moses-es law should be observed; for righteousness-es sake Jesus-es teaching is to be followed." Believe it or not, the correct oral form is: "For conscience sake, Moses law should be observed; for righteousness sake, Jesus teaching is to be followed." The correct punctuation of this sentence is as follows: "For conscience' sake, Moses' law should be observed; for righteousness' sake, Jesus' teaching is to be followed." Be aware, however, that this rule of English is rather obscure (even if very useful) and is more frequently disregarded than obeyed—even by radio and television announcers or in theological schools and pulpits.

But now we must address more basic issues.

Lines 1-2. Unless the prayer leader has indicated before beginning that there is to be a prayer related to the public referendum, the listener must wait too long to discover what this prayer is about. The phrase "the matter before us this week" is vague. "The referendum before us this week" reveals the subject of the prayer more readily.

Lines 3-6. Remember that the slogan of the pro-tax party is "Property ownership implies public responsibility." Therefore the phrase "the responsibility we have" will immediately be heard as a speech in favor of the tax increase, whether the leader of prayer intends it that way or not. The seeming bias of the leader is increased in line 4: "selfish motives that cause us to consider our own pocketbooks ahead of the public good" seems to be an attack on the anti-tax people (who undoubtedly have been charged with being selfish for opposing the referendum). And lines 5-6 intensify the problem. The property owners who oppose the tax increase will feel they are being chastised as "persons of privilege" who are being called upon to "sacrifice" "for the benefit of everyone" in ways not expected of those who do not own property. Hence lines 3-6 appear to have a very partisan flavor.

Lines 7-11. Some sentences should never have been written, and this is one of them. It is grammatically complex and cannot be read easily even by a leader. (Never should such a sentence be used in a unison prayer.) My attempts to rewrite it are not to be taken as an ideal reconstruction. But that aside, there are major problems of content as well as form. This sentence is not as seemingly partisan as lines 3-6, although the existence of lines 3-6 can make lines 7-11 appear more one-sided than they are. But lines 7-11 fall into the trap of a nationalism that can be at odds with the gospel. Do the values of Christianity allow American Christians to say with a straight face that our democracy treats all equally? As a direct quotation from the pledge to the U.S. flag, "one nation under God" is the language of political speeches, not prayer. (Remember: There may be in the congregation Christian citizens of other countries, who also wish to be able to say the amen at the end of the prayer.)

Then in **lines 11-13** theological problems are added to political problems due to words that seem to equate the task of public education with that of Christian education. Is it the proper function of the public schools to cause all students to "submit" to the will and way of Jesus? Or is it the congregation's program of Christian teaching that exists for the purpose of making disciples of people?

Given these problems, I encourage the writer of this prayer to begin again. A suitable reconstruction might look like this:

O God, our Source and Sovereign,
to you we come with our confusion and divergent views
*   on the referendum before us this week.*
Show us how best we may promote the welfare

of everyone within our community,
despite our varied personal interests
and our often contradictory opinions.

Enable each of us to seek the greatest good for all of us.
Cause us to approach the ballot box with open hearts and minds,
    seeking to know your will in the decision we must make.
Clothe us with prayer, thoughtfulness, and graciousness
    as we enter the voting booth.

We bless you for the teachers and administrators of our schools,
    and we remember the generations before them
    who have prepared their way.
Fill us with gracious words and generous deeds
    by which to encourage our public educators
    and assist them in their task.
Strengthen their labors for the good
    of the community, the nation, and the world.

Show us who are within the church
    how best we may carry out
    the particular responsibility you have given to us
    as a community of faith
to spread the gospel and to make disciples
    by teaching others in our church schools
    through compelling word and faithful witness.

To all of us in community and church,
    grant wisdom in our work
    and fulfillment as the fruit of our labors.
This we pray through Jesus Christ,
    who is divine Wisdom among us and for us.

The Sounds and Silence of Public Prayer

The church cannot say amen to words the church cannot hear. Problems related to adequate and accurate hearing are numerous and need to be examined under two headings: the natural voice of the speaker and the augmented voice, which is assisted by technology. Then we shall look at the other sounds we may encounter at prayer and at the use of silence in the praying assembly.

The natural voice of the leader refers to the human voice not amplified by electronic means and free of distortion caused by the acoustics of the building. Even in an intimate setting with no acoustical problems, words can readily be lost if the speech becomes too soft or rapid—or if articulation is indistinct so that words run together or entire syllables disappear. Spoken too rapidly, "let us pray" can sound like "lettuce spray." Most church people probably will not notice because the invitation to prayer is so familiar the ear compensates for the error. But you get the point. Each word needs to be said distinctly, with particular attention being given to the sounding out of the consonants and to adequate separation between words. In rooms with poor acoustics this is even more crucial than in rooms that are acoustically favorable to the spoken voice.

The leader in prayer may be in trouble if "Teach us to follow your will, and enable us to serve others in all ways open to us" comes out sounding like: "Tea jus to fowl ya will, anaybul us to sir vothers in always opatus." Granted, certain regional habits of speaking may prevail; if the speaker and the listener share the same speech patterns the problem will be reduced—except for visitors from other regions. But in many instances speech that is indistinct and difficult to understand springs from a lazy tongue rather than from established and shared speech patterns. The congregation that cannot determine what the leader is saying quickly abandons the attempt. The *amen* fails to be said with integrity (or perhaps at all) because the leader has not taken leadership seriously.

The maintenance of adequate volume is also critical, and herein lies one of the most serious defects of many public speakers. In English, as in many languages, we signal the end of a thought by a slight decline in the pitch of the voice. This is so ingrained you probably have never even stopped to think about it until now. But mentally consider the difference in sound between the two statements that follow:

"It looks like it is going to rain." [An assertion.]

"It looks like it is going to rain?" [An incredulous reply when someone has made this assertion under a cloudless sky.]

At the close of the assertion the voice pitch declines, while at the end of the reply the voice pitch ascends. Normally among public speakers (including those who are at prayer) pitch declines slightly at the end of a sentence, more deeply at the end of a paragraph, and even more noticeably at the very close of the remarks. But what does this have to do with volume? Far more than you may think.

For all too often even in conversation, when the pitch of the voice drops so does the volume. In his autobiography, Walter Cronkite tells the amusing story of sitting next to Jacquelyn Kennedy Onassis at dinner one evening while she was relating to him what he thought must be a very revealing instance in her life with the late president. But at the end of every sentence the volume of Jackie's voice dropped so drastically that Cronkite had no real notion as to what she was trying to tell him; after two attempts to get her to repeat it with sustained volume, he gave up![13] Cronkite never knew what anecdote about Kennedy he missed thereby. The experience is all too common even among lesser mortals. You have probably heard sermons in which the last sentence or two was uttered so softly you could not decipher it—this despite the fact that the closing words may have been crucial, and the preacher may have spent a great deal of time in selecting them.

The link between decline in pitch and decline in volume seems to be a natural one. It is sometimes referred to as "the double dip," and it is a bond public speakers must work overtime to break. Even the world's best public address system cannot amplify what does not exist. If you have the problem of declining volume (and it will take some honest people in the congregation to tell you, even if you ask), try this: When you are alone around the house or in your car, practice again and again the art of lowering pitch without reducing volume.

An overly rapid rate of delivery is also an enemy of those who speak in public, particularly because it is readily induced by anxiety. To the nervous speaker, time seems to drag. ("Come on, let's get this over with and get out of here" is the mind's subconscious message to the voice.) Thus the delivery may speed up to the point that the listener can barely follow. While we rarely stop to think about it, speaking and listening are acts of encoding and decoding. For languages are codes we humans use in attempts to express ourselves. The problem of rapidity is actually a double one: If the code comes too rapidly, the brain of the listener may have difficulty even recognizing its sounds—at the very point when that brain is required to do decoding in a reduced amount of time. The listener eventually becomes wearied.

With regard to the pacing of prayer, there is another factor to be noted. While prayer should never drag to the point of tedium, it should be slightly slower than conversation, so that worshipers can ponder or even silently repeat the key words before God as a way of participating actively. Therefore even the normal rate of speech, unaccelerated by anxiety, may need to be slowed slightly.

Fortunately, careful attention to the articulation of words tends to be a self-correcting measure in relation to the problem of rapidity. Most people cannot carefully articulate all consonants and also tear along at break-neck speed. (Recall the "Peter Piper picked a peck of pickled peppers" phenomenon: The more quickly you say it, the more confused it becomes.) But if you have excellent articulation and still discover you are speaking too rapidly, you may need to practice deliberation by continually reminding yourself that time is not dragging nearly as much as you think it is. Occasionally the opposite problem occurs. People speak too slowly, often because they are unprepared and are trying to figure out what to say next. This causes no problem in the decoding process, though it may cause the listener to want to reach down the throat of the speaker and pull the words out.

Some persons who are inexperienced at leading in public prayer find it useful to position in the rear of the room someone who will give prearranged hand signals indicating a need to articulate, to increase the volume, and to slow or accelerate the pace. If this assistance puts you at greater ease during your earliest leadership experiences, feel free to arrange for it.

In many instances, the voice of the speaker will be augmented by use of a public address system. Like so many things in life, a public address system can at once be a blessing or a curse. Well modulated and monitored by a person who understands its operation, the PA system can overcome the limitations of the human voice and many defects in a building's acoustical properties. Poorly designed or operated, the PA system can crackle and pop, emit ear-shattering squeals, pick up extraneous noises from radio stations and CB enthusiasts, or simply seem to do nothing whatsoever.

If you are to use an amplification system, it is mandatory that you rehearse with it and its operator. Some systems have no operator, in which case you yourself may be expected to learn how to regulate the controls. Not having done so in advance will only add to your anxiety when the time of leadership arrives. Therefore become as familiar as possible with the equipment before the day on which you are to use it. Above all, know how to shut the system down if that becomes necessary.

Microphones vary greatly in their characteristics. Some pick up a wide range of sounds and magnify them indiscriminately, so that the turning of pages may produce distracting rustling noises. Other microphones are designed to pick up sounds only within a couple of inches; the sounds of turning pages will not be picked up—but neither will the human voice if the speaker is too far from the microphone. In particular, a cordless hand-held mike is utterly useless if the speaker gestures generously with the hand holding the microphone, thereby moving it well away from the lips.

You may be asked to wear a tiny clip-on microphone; it will be connected by a cord to a regulating apparatus that you place in a pocket or attach to your belt. You may be instructed to turn this apparatus on immediately before you begin to speak and to turn it off when finished. Failure to observe these instructions has frequently resulted in great embarrassment, as remarks thought to be audible only to someone nearby suddenly were broadcast loudly to everyone present. Therefore it is mandatory, not merely advisable, that you learn the proper operation of the equipment before using it during a worship service.

Occasionally a public address device will act in unanticipated ways. Often the speakers from which amplified sound emits are placed on the walls or ceiling well in front of the podium or pulpit. This helps to prevent the objectionable shrieks of "feedback" that can occur when the sound coming out of these speakers is fed back into the microphone, only to be amplified again—and again and again. But the location of the audio speakers some distance in front of the person at the microphone means this leader may not hear things the listeners hear. Once, during an announcement period, a parishioner yelled out to me, "Take that microphone off. We can hear you better without it." A clip-on microphone was attached to my tie. The jacket and shirt I was wearing were producing slight pops of static electricity, generated as the fabrics rubbed against each other. These sounds, almost inaudible to me, were being projected to the congregation with distracting magnification.

But sometimes it is not advisable to take or turn the microphone off. You need to know ahead of time what the mike is doing. Is it merely amplifying for the sake of those with normal hearing? Or is it also assisting persons who are hard of hearing by means of an "FM loop" transmission to earphones such persons are using? It may be broadcasting the service through a local radio station, or recording the service on a tape cassette later to be shared with shut-in members. Then the microphone cannot be shunned, even if your voice is strong enough to carry well to all parts of the room without amplification.

There are sounds associated with prayer other than that of the spoken voice. A prayer may be sung by a soloist or choir, for example. The singing voice is even more likely to present challenges to the listener than the spoken voice. If the words are indistinct, the congregation has great difficulty following the text, let alone regarding it as a prayer in which they join. In many instances it is advisable to print in the service folder for the day the texts to be sung.

Too often such a musical selection is regarded simply as a kind of musical interlude inserted between various spoken acts. This unfortunately causes many worshipers to regard themselves for that moment as an audience to be entertained rather than as a congregation of Christ's people at prayer. At times it may be helpful to introduce such music by saying "We continue to pray as the choir offers petitions to God on our behalf" or "The anthem is a prayer in which all of us join silently."

Nor should it be overlooked that many things we regard simply as hymns are indeed acts of thanksgiving, praise, lament, confession, or petition. A well-planned service of worship is not a variety show into which hymns are inserted from time to time to keep the people alert or to allow them to stand up and stretch. A well-planned service has a rationale. But often this fact is obscured.

Suppose that the opening hymn is an act of petition or of pure praise to the Almighty, such as "Our [or, O] God, Our Help in Ages Past" and "Holy, Holy, Holy," respectively. In both of these texts, all words are addressed directly to God. Therefore, it may be a bit misleading to introduce a spoken prayer immediately after the hymn with the words, "Let us pray." The implication is, "The opening hymn was not a prayer." The more apt introduction may be "As we have praised God in sung prayer, so now we continue to praise God in speech, saying. . . ." The idealistic side of me objects to this as being too pedantic and prefers the simpler "Let us pray." But the realistic side of me knows that many worshipers operate on automatic pilot unless someone occasionally prods the brain cells into thinking about what is actually happening within the order of service.

There are numerous liturgical functions that hymns can perform. A few hymns are in fact litanies—a series of petitions to which a common response is added. Such a hymn is "For the Beauty of the Earth." The point is made if a soloist or choir sings the stanzas and the rest of the worshiping assembly sings only the refrain. The bulletin may even contain this entry: "Sung Litany of Thanksgiving." Other hymn texts are prayers of confession: "Pass Me Not, O Gentle Savior," "Rock of Ages," and "Forgive Our Sins as We Forgive" are in this category. One of these can be used as the day's confession after an introduction such as: "In song rather than speech, let us make our humble confession of sin to God." If the people normally sit or kneel for confession, retain that use of posture during the singing. If substituting sung confession for spoken confession is not desirable, a hymn of confession is best sung immediately before the spoken confession, or following it but preceding any assurance or declaration of pardon. Placing such a hymn at some other point in the service may obscure what the text means, causing it to be regarded simply as musical relief from whatever else has been going on.

In addition to prayer that is spoken or sung, there is prayer uttered silently. Typically a time of silence is allowed for personal confession after the corporate confession has been said or sung. On occasion, the intercessions may consist of a sequence of periods of silence, with the topics for silent prayer being directed by a leader (see exercise 20). The besetting sin of such practices is that the leader (usually driven by an anxious determination as discussed above) does not allow enough time for the people to engage in their silent prayers. More often than not, I am barely able to begin my prayer in silence before the leader interrupts me by moving on to the next item. Knowing how much time is enough is an art in itself. To a congregation not accustomed to silence, thirty seconds may seem like an eternity. But little can be said to God in fewer than fifteen or twenty seconds.

For good reason, an entire minute or more of silence may be observed. (Remember the funeral of Princess Diana?) But it is well to introduce such a period explicitly: "In memory of all who have died during the past year, it is our custom each All Saints Sunday to keep sixty seconds of silence.) Otherwise, worshipers tend to fidget and speculate as to whether the prayer leader has fallen asleep. This fact may amuse members of the Society of Friends; but most mainline Protestants would not make very good Quakers, and we must face that realistically. In many congregations, it may be well to increase the length of silence over several months so that those unaccustomed to such periods can adjust to them gradually. It is also beneficial to encourage people to engage in silent prayer and meditation at home.

This brings us to the issue of unwanted and unplanned sounds while we are at prayer. Sixty seconds of silence can be horrendously disrupted when the siren on the fire house across the street suddenly sounds five seconds into the period. It will be still worse if volunteer fire fighters spring up all over the congregation and dash out of the door. Less obtrusive but still disruptive will be crying children and persons who cannot stifle a cough or sneeze—and become greatly embarrassed because they cannot, perhaps to the point of not returning to worship services again for fear of repeating the behavior. The leader of prayer should first of all avoid doing anything to further embarrass such a worshiper. Usually the best strategy is to call no attention to the behavior. To glare at a parent whose child is unruly is at least as rude as failing to move the child to another location (if indeed one can be found). But even to say a well meant *"Gesundheit"* or "God bless you" to someone who has sneezed may humiliate the person more than is already the case.

In a few instances the disruptions may be somewhat predictable. I once served as pastor of a congregation whose building was set on a hill; several times every Sunday during our services, a city bus noisily shifted into a lower gear just outside the worship space. I tried to plan the order of service around the published bus schedule; but, frankly, it worked only sporadically.

Occasionally a noisy disruption may actually introduce an occasion for prayer. In a certain church building located very near an emergency medical center, the worship hour is from time to time interrupted by ambulances with sirens wailing so loudly that it is wise simply to suspend the service for a few moments. Before resuming a sermon in this congregation, its preacher takes the occasion to offer a brief prayer for the person in distress and for all who are giving medical attention. Or if it is a prayer that is interrupted, the same petition is inserted when the prayer resumes.

Over the past several decades there has been a waning of the custom, once popular among Protestants, of having soft organ or other instrumental music throughout a time of prayer, particularly if the praying was done in silence. Presumably this background music toned down minor noises within the congregation. But it also tended to create the impression that praying is a kind of ethereal, other-worldly activity. (All too often, organists engaged a vibrato stop, which gave the impression of angels humming nearby.) Prayer is intimate conversation with God carried on in the real world, to which music can itself be a distraction, particularly if a familiar hymn tune causes the words of the hymn to take over our minds to the detriment of our prayer.

Those who plan and lead worship will not be able to insulate the congregation from every distraction; but they should creatively consider how best to use both the sounds and the silences to enhance effective corporate prayer.

Constructing a Thematic Prayer Based on Scripture

Read Psalm 133.

In contrast to the comprehensive prayer considered in exercise 15, a thematic prayer deals with one subject, likely viewed from a variety of angles. Later in this exercise I am going to ask you to write a thematic prayer such as might be used at a conference on world peace sponsored by a group of churches. There is no way I can look over what you have done in the writing of that prayer. The best I can do is to provide you with two aids:

1. I will ask you to look over my shoulder as I construct a thematic prayer on a different theme—that of racial harmony and justice.

2. I will then provide a checklist you can use after you have written your own prayer; much on that list will serve as a review to what you have done in the previous exercises.

Suppose now that I have been asked to offer a prayer at the opening of an ecumenical conference on racial harmony and justice. Because I believe that in such a setting the most effective prayers are those that are anchored in the Scriptures, I will begin by recalling passages of scripture related to the theme. Immediately there comes to mind Acts 17:26— "From one ancestor he [God] made all nations to inhabit the whole earth." To be honest, this is a tricky passage; while it is the first one to leap to my mind, it is not without problems. What follows immediately in the passage has often been used by bigots to justify segregation and racial "purity" ("and he allotted the times of their existence and the boundaries of the places where they would live"). But read further and Luke (the author of the Acts) asserts that we are all God's offspring, an affirmation that corrects a discriminatory misreading of the text.

Also, I am quickly reminded of another passage in the Acts: Peter's realization that "God shows no partiality, but in every nation anyone who fears him and does what is right is acceptable to him" (Acts 10:34-35). I also recall Paul's teaching that "There is no longer Jew or Greek, there is no longer slave or free, there is no longer male and female; for all of you are one in Christ Jesus" (Galatians 3:28). And I remember the words of Ephesians concerning Jews and Gentiles: "[Christ] has made both groups into one and has broken down the dividing wall, that is, the hostility between us, that he might create in himself one new humanity in place of two, thus making peace, and might reconcile both groups to God in one body through the cross" (Ephesians 2:14-16).

I also ponder how often Jesus in his ministry and teaching overrode the traditional hostility between Jews and Samaritans. At the well, he talked to a Samaritan, and a woman at that (John 4:1-30). He made a Samaritan the hero of his parable about the man who fell into the hands of robbers (Luke 10:30-37). He deliberately traveled through Samaria with his disciples, when most devout Jews carefully bypassed Samaritan territory (John 4:4). And he took due note of the fact that of ten persons whom he healed of the same disease, only one returned to give thanks—one who was a Samaritan (Luke 17:11-19). I also recall Jesus' teaching about the heavenly banquet at which they "will come from east and west, from north and south, and will eat in the kingdom of God" (Luke 13:29).

Furthermore, the writer of the Revelation reports seeing in heaven "a great multitude that no one could count, from every nation, from all tribes and peoples and languages, standing before the throne" (Revelation 7:9). And the gates of heaven are never shut, so that all may freely enter (Revelation 21:25-26).

Of course I also recall Psalm 133, which you read at the beginning of this section. I remember that Jonah, a Jew, was sent to a Gentile city, Nineveh, to preach repentance. And when the people repented, God received them gladly, although Jonah's prejudice and pride made this a problem for him. And the book of Ruth closes by telling us (subtly but insistently) that David, considered the greatest monarch of the Jews, had in his veins the blood of Ruth, his Gentile great-grandmother.

As you can tell, the task of drawing on biblical resources becomes easier as you learn more and more of the content of the Bible. I am grateful for all of the exercises of memorizing scripture that were thrust upon me when I was a lad in Sunday school, and I lament the fact that committing Bible passages to memory has become unfashionable in many circles within the church. If you do not know the Bible well, a good concordance or Bible search program on your computer can be a great assistance. But nothing will suffice you so fully as learning the content of the Scriptures better.

Pondering now all of the above, and considering carefully the purposes of the conference at which I am to lead in prayer, I constructed the following prayer. Words *in italics* are quotations of, or allusions to, scripture; the biblical sources are indicated in the right margin.

Holy God, creator of the universe and our maker: *From one ancestor you have made every nation on earth. Before your heavenly throne stand multitudes from every nation, from all tribes and peoples and languages. For you show no partiality. In every nation anyone who does what is right is acceptable to you.*

Acts 17:26

Revelation 7:9
Acts 10:34-35

We confess with shame that it is otherwise with us. We do not adequately reflect *your image and likeness, in which you have made us.* We separate ourselves with *dividing walls,* and make virtue of *the hostility between us.* We prefer those who look like us and agree with us; we fear those who are different. Like *Jonah at Nineveh* we even may resent your kindness toward those we dislike. And within the fellowship of the church, which Christ *reconciled in one body through the cross,* we divide what he united by the *offering of his own life* and *the power of his resurrection.*

Genesis 1:26

Ephesians 2:14-16
Jonah 3–4

Ephesians 2:16
Hebrews 10:10; Philippians 3:10

Have mercy upon us, that we may live and praise you as *one new humanity,* transformed by your grace. Enable us to live as those who are *one in Christ Jesus,* and cause us to embody the respect and love he demonstrated to *Samaritans* and *Gentiles,* to those who were *low and despised in the world.* Give us a zeal to *do justice,* a passion for *loving kindness, and* a determination to show *humility as we walk with you in obedience to the truth through the Spirit.*

Ephesians 2:15
Galatians 3:28
(Various texts)
1 Corinthians 1:28

Micah 6:8
1 Peter 1:22

We remember with gratitude all who have given unselfishly of themselves in the cause of justice and racial understanding, even to the point of *laying down their lives;* of them *the world was not worthy.* We give thanks also for those who work tirelessly to unite *east and west, north and south,* that your people may know *how good and pleasant it is to live together in unity.*

John 15:13
Hebrews 11:38
Luke 13:29
Psalm 133:1

As we meet together to pursue racial harmony and justice, make us *strong and let our hearts take courage as we wait for you* to show your power among us. *Take away our hearts of stone and give us hearts of flesh.* Put away from us pessimism, fault-finding, and unbending points of view. In their stead give us *patience, kindness, generosity, faithfulness, and gentleness, the fruit of your Spirit.* Prosper our work, that we may present to you not only

Psalm 27:14

Ezekiel 36:26

Galatians 5:22

our repentance, but the true *fruits of a repentance* that *leads to salvation and brings no regret.*

    This we ask in the name of him who invites to his heavenly banquet *Jew and Greek, slave and free, male and female,* Jesus Christ, *the cornerstone in whom all is joined together.*

Matthew 3:8
2 Corinthians 7:10

Galatians 3:28
Ephesians 2:20-21

As I worked through this prayer, I decided not to use some of the biblical passages I had thought about originally. And I added in many other quotations and allusions. Some of these occurred from memory; at other points I relied on a concordance for ideas.

Now begin to plan your own prayer, designed for an ecumenical conference on world peace. Some of the passages I have used you may also wish to employ. (Fortunately there is no copyright on the use of Scripture when at prayer!) But search your mind and use concordance tools to call up other ideas. Your prayer need not be as long as mine; even so, likely you will not want to try to do the entire prayer in one sitting. Much is gained by brooding over time, and your subconscious mind will be working on this process when you are exercising, fixing dinner, or even sleeping. Please do not proceed in the reading of material in this exercise until you have fully completed at least a first draft of your prayer.

Now, having written your prayer, pause to think about the process of putting it together. What facets of world peace and justice came into your mind, and how did you relate these to the mission of the church? What biblical passages related to these themes did you discover, whether from memory or through the use of concordances and similar aids? Reflecting on the process through which you worked can help you as you construct similar prayers for the future.

Now some specifics:

1. Read through your prayer and honestly face the question: "Have I kept a firm focus on the subject of world peace and justice, or have I introduced extraneous items?" Such items may well be justified in a prayer for a *different* occasion, even though detracting from the unity of the prayer for *this* occasion. Those who lead in public prayer need a clear sense of what is appropriate to each occasion.

2. With a colored pen, circle or highlight every verb of petition. Then read only the verbs aloud in sequence. Have you used vigorous verbs (for example, *strengthen, enlighten, transform, undergird*) or anemic verbs and phrases, such as "be with" and "we pray for/that"? Replace any anemic words you find with verbs that are bold. (As necessary, review exercise 5 for assistance.)

3. Again go through the prayer and underline any occurrences of wishful thinking: "may we," "let us," "if only we would," and such. Replace these words addressed to the congregation with verbs of petition addressed to God. (Again, review exercise 5 as needed.)

4. Once more go over the prayer and cross through all words that do no work: "we just want to," "we come to you asking," "we pray that you would," and so on. Rephrase the prayer as necessary to make it read smoothly after the deletions. (Consult exercise 6 for suggestions.)

5. Examine the language of the prayer to see if it seems to exclude any persons or groups (see exercise 13). Note that exclusion can spring from words people do not understand. For example, at a conference on peace, it is tempting to use the term *shalom*; but if some people present do not know that word, they will be puzzled, even annoyed, and may feel excluded. If you have formal training in theology, be alert to phrases you may know well but which are meaningless to those without such training: examples include *eschatological hope, ecclesial concerns, salvific grace,* and *ethical imperative.*

6. Now look carefully at the prayer to see what it implies negatively about the God to whom we pray. Strike out those phrases that suggest the absence of God: (a) multiple uses of the divine name; (b) requests that God should "come and be present with us"; (c) talking *about* God rather than *to* God; (e) using the word "might" as a present tense verb. We have already edited two other pesky components of "The Absent Deity Syndrome": "be with" and "may we/ let us" constructions. (Review exercise 11 as necessarily for clarification.)

7. Now look at what the prayer implies positively about the God to whom we pray. What attributes of God are mentioned? (See exercise 8.) Suppose someone who knew nothing at all about the Christian faith visited the conference for which you have written this prayer; as a result of the ways in which you have spoken to God, what impression would the visitor take away concerning the nature of God?

8. Now write a revised draft of the prayer.

9. Read the new draft aloud. Are any sentences so long that they are difficult to speak with grace and ease? Are there combinations of words that seem awkward? You may wish to read the prayer aloud to another person in order to get a second opinion. Once more, revise as necessary.

Exercise 18

Praying Outside the Church (Interreligious Settings)

Read Psalm 150.

Our consideration thus far has been confined to prayer within the Christian community of faith. "Christian community" here is broadly defined to include all who share a common faith in the God made known through Jesus Christ. This can include Roman Catholic, Protestant, and Orthodox Christians; such groups of worshipers are correctly called "ecumenical," and when leading in prayer in such a group we are fully "within the church." But there will be occasions for leading in prayer in settings where those present espouse religions other than Christianity—or none at all. It is these settings that come under the category of "praying outside the church." Our discussion here is of gatherings constituted by a mixture of Jews, Muslims, Christians, and perhaps other faiths. These gatherings are properly called *interfaith*, not *ecumenical*; however, the two terms are often used incorrectly. Hence if you are invited to lead prayers at either "an ecumenical gathering" or an "interfaith gathering," you need specifically to ask whether this assembly is of Christians only, or of persons from various other faiths as well.

Prayer settings "outside of the church" fall into two principal categories: (1) the intentionally religious setting and (2) the incidentally religious setting. The meaning of these terms will be made clear as we go along.

(1) An interfaith occasion that is intentionally religious most likely will be a worship service cosponsored by a number of local churches, synagogues, mosques, and similar established institutions. The marriage service for a Christian and a Jew is also an interfaith occasion, though whether it is intentionally religious or only incidentally so will depend upon the religious commitments of the bride and groom.

In an intentionally religious setting, it can be assumed that those who attend come expecting to participate in a variety of acts of worship, including prayer. Any such service should be jointly planned by knowledgeable representatives (laity or clergy) of each sponsoring group. Very quickly in the discussion, the matter of how to pray together will surely arise.

For example, (a) the Jews may say to the Christians, "It would be well for you not to use any specifically Christian language in your prayers so that we Jews will not feel excluded and so that we heartily can join in the amen. (b) Or, on the contrary, the Jews may say, "By all means, pray from within your own tradition, as we will from within ours. If you fail to do this, we who are Jewish will feel that we are being patronized or at least that we are unduly constraining your authentic piety." Early within the planning process, these two differing approaches should be discussed and one or the other chosen. Here are the options more fully described.

(a) The first approach asserts that the service is to be planned and written in such a way that at every point all present can affirm the content. (Actual amens may or may not be used, depending upon which religious groups are being included in the worshiping assembly.) This obviously means that a Christian leading in prayer will not pray "through Jesus Christ our Lord," or use trinitarian or other distinctively Christian language. If this first approach is chosen, all portions of the service should be written out well in advance and approved for use by the appointed representatives of each sponsoring body.

(b) An alternative possibility within an intentionally religious setting is this. Anything to be said or sung by all present should conform to the standards mentioned in the previous paragraph; but individual leaders of the service when acting on their own are to maintain the integrity of their specific traditions. Thus no hymns or unison prayers include references to Christ, for example; but a prayer spoken by an individual Christian would properly make such references, just as a prayer spoken by a Muslim would include the name of Allah. Under the terms of this approach, not everyone present is expected to affirm each prayer; for worshipers are there not only to pray together at some points but also to learn about traditions distinct from their own. Some intentionally interfaith services cosponsored by a variety of religious communities are designed on this principle.

This second approach within an intentionally religious setting also often pertains at a wedding between, let us say, a Christian woman and a Unitarian man who considers himself to be a theist but not a Christian. The couple may agree, for example, that the groom will declare his intention to his wife simply "in the name of God," while the bride in the corresponding vow will declare to her husband that she is marrying him "in the name of the Father, and of the Son, and of the Holy Spirit." But no congregational hymns or unison prayers will make reference to the Trinity. Both parties to the marriage thus retain the integrity of their respective traditions without requiring that the other party or any of the wedding guests embrace that tradition. Alternatively, in such an instance the prospective bride and groom may decide to use the first approach, so that no specifically Christian references are used at any time in the service. Which of the approaches to choose is a matter the couple will have to deliberate with care, for the outcome likely will be the precedent for many such decisions they will have to make in establishing an interfaith household.

In all cases of services that are intentionally religious, it is crucial that one of these two approaches to interfaith worship be firmly decided upon and that the actual language to be used at a service be put in writing well in advance. To postpone such decisions until the day (or even the week) before the service is to court disaster. It may even be that in the course of preliminary discussions concerning the event, an impasse is reached, causing one or more of the prospective participants to withdraw from participation—or, in the extreme, causing the entire service to be scrapped. Tragic as such an outcome may be, it is easier if this occurs several months before the planned event rather than on the eve of it.

On the brighter side, agreements may arise that are unexpected. Once, while carrying out the responsibility for writing and coordinating a rite for a Christian-Jewish service, I was astounded to discover that an eminent rabbi participating in the planning consented readily to the unison use of the New Testament prayer that begins "Our Father in heaven, hallowed be your name"—so long as it was not referred to as "The Lord's Prayer." He explained: "It is obvious that we Jews do not regard Jesus as our Lord. Still, everything within that prayer is totally consonant with the teachings of our Jewish Scriptures. We have no difficulty with the content, only with the title." And so in the service bulletin the heading read simply "Prayer," with the further instruction that it was to be said by all present. But other rabbis would disallow the unison use of this prayer at an interreligious gathering on this assumption: Traditional practice has so closely linked this prayer to the life of the church that it is "distinctively Christian" by psychological association, if not by theological content.

Incidentally, when the prayer in Matthew 6:9-13 is deemed acceptable for use by all parties at an interfaith event, probably it is best to employ a contemporary translation. Without *art, thy,* and *thine,* the prayer is somewhat less wedded to traditional Christian usage and thus may seem more comfortable for persons of other faiths.

As the discussion above suggests, the planning situation for each interfaith event will be different, if only because so much depends upon the personalities of those engaged in the process. It is not possible to devise a "one size fits all" formula, even for something as relatively simple as a prayer service only for Christians and Jews or a Jewish-Christian wedding. Add in Muslims, Shintoist, Bahias, and various other groups, and the necessity for tailoring each service separately should be evident. Furthermore, almost all religious traditions are fractured; hence approaches will differ depending upon whether the participating Jews are Orthodox, Conservative, Reform, or Reconstructionist, or whether Islamic representatives are Sunni, Sufi, Shi'ite, or Black Muslim.

(2) Now we come to the other (and usually more common) category: settings that are only incidentally religious. That is, the gathering is not primarily religious in nature, but prayer is desired, most likely at the beginning or end (or both). For example, you are asked to lead a prayer at a convention of sales representatives, a meeting of the DAR, the centennial celebration of a city, a retirement dinner, or the inauguration of a community college president. None of these constitutes a religious event as such, and it should not be assumed that people come actually intending to pray; at least, they do not regard prayer to be a primary reason for their gathering. Prayer in such a setting is thought of as incidental to the main event. This fact complicates the situation discussed under "intentionally religious settings."

First of all, in addition to the possible presence of persons from many religious persuasions, in such a setting there may well be agnostics and atheists. Not only do these persons come without the intention of praying; they may be quite alienated because they feel trapped in a situation not of their own making. Assuming this is a not a government sanctioned event (which would add complicating questions about the separation of church and state), the presence of such dissenters should not necessarily prevent prayer by those who wish to participate. But at least a gracious introduction to the act of prayer can be given. Instead of the familiar injunction, "Let us pray," the leader can begin by saying, "I invite all who wish to participate in prayer to join in these words addressed to God." Never should an invitation to prayer either in word choice or tone of voice suggest disparagement of those who prefer not to enter into the devotional act. The graciousness of God should be made manifest to the fullest possible extent. (For their part, dissenters should maintain a quiet demeanor, showing no disrespect or rudeness toward those who do wish to join in prayer.)

A further complication to the incidentally religious occasion is this: Often those who are responsible for placing prayer on the agenda of a convention, business meeting, or civic celebration give little thought to why they wish to include such an act. "We just felt it might be a nice thing to do," they may respond, if the person asked to lead in prayer inquires into the rationale. And often the planners have given no thought to the interfaith composition of those who will attend. Most likely being Christians themselves (whether profoundly so or superficially so), they may see nothing improper about asking a Christian to lead Jews, Muslims, and atheists in prayer. Indeed, they may be only dimly aware that such persons will be present. Occasionally they will plan to have two prayers, one fore and aft of whatever the group is basically gathered to do; but even this does not guarantee that they will invite both a Christian and a Jew to lead the respective prayers. As often as not, they will ask one Catholic and one Protestant, or perhaps invite the same person to offer both prayers. (To those who set the agenda and invite you to participate, Orthodox Christians are usually as psychologically invisible as Muslims and Buddhists.)

Therefore if you are being asked to lead the prayers of such an assemblage, you will need to press for clarity as to the assignment; but also you will need to be prepared to receive less clarification about your task than you might like to have and certainly less than you would receive from the planners of an interfaith event that is intentionally religious. If you discover you are the only person being asked to lead in prayer, it is perfectly proper for you to suggest that a person of another faith also be invited to participate; even if only Christians show up at the event, it is beneficial that they thus be made aware of the presence in society (if not in the same room) of varied expressions of faith and prayer.

If you are one of at least two persons from differing traditions, then those who are leading will need to discuss among themselves the same issues mentioned concerning intentionally religious events: Will the Christian pray as a Christian, and the Muslim as a Muslim? Or will both offer prayers that suggest none of the distinctiveness of either faith so that all present may say the amen to each prayer? At times you may legitimately be the only person asked to lead in prayer, when you know persons of other faiths are present. This may most likely occur at a dinner party—a typical example of an event that is incidentally religious—and one at which you may find yourself saying grace with little or no warning.

At a minimum, in such circumstances in which you offer the prayer in the name of all present, some of whom are persons of other faiths, you will be gracious enough to delete specifically Christian references. If you are familiar with the prayer forms of the others who are present, and if these are consonant with your own beliefs, inclusion of such forms is eminently appropriate. When Jews are present, for example, instead of closing the prayer "through Christ our Savior" the familiar Jewish prayer formula, "Blessed are you, O Lord our God, ruler of the universe," may be substituted to the approbation of all present.

The final verse of the book of Psalms exhorts: "Let everything that breathes praise the Lord." As a prayer leader, your task is to lead in prayer in ways that can enable all who breathe to join in common praise and petition. (But be warned that some very conservative Christians will object to this inclusive approach; for they feel it their duty to pray only through Jesus Christ and their obligation to convert all others to Christianity.)

Now let's try editing a prayer for an incidentally religious occasion, the inauguration of a mayor. In most communities it will be assumed that church-state issues do not prevent such prayer, and usually prayer has been included in the event for as long as the community has been inaugurating mayors.

1   You, O God, are the ruler of the universe and our maker. We know that you gather your people

2   together in communities for mutual support and the pursuit of the common good. In our system

3   of government we democratically select those who govern us. As Paul the Apostle has told us:

4   God has called us to live together in harmony with one another. Therefore on this occasion we

5   put aside party loyalties and join together in the joy of this event. We ask that God would guide

6   Mauveen as she assumes the office of mayor. May all of her decisions be made with a view to the

7   welfare of all. We desire that she may govern with honesty, integrity, and justice. May we work

8   with her administration for the benefit of our city according to biblical teaching. Grant this for

9   the sake of your righteous name.

Do not proceed to the next page until you have completed your editing of the above prayer.

Suggested Revisions and Commentary

1   You, O God, are the ruler of the universe and our maker. ~~We know that you~~ **You** gather your people

2   together in communities for mutual support and the pursuit of the common good. ~~In our system~~ **We give thanks**

3   ~~of government we democratically select~~ **for the privilege and responsibility of selecting** those who govern us. ~~As Paul the Apostle has told us:~~ **Enable us, despite our varied**

4   ~~God has called us~~ **gifts and circumstances,** to live together in harmony ~~with one another. Therefore on this occasion we~~ **Give us grace to**

5   put aside party loyalties and join together in the joy of this event. ~~We ask that God would guide~~ **Guide**

6   Mauveen as she assumes the office of mayor. ~~May~~ **Enable her to make** all of her decisions ~~be made~~ with a view to the

7   welfare of all. ~~We desire that she may~~ **Strengthen her to** govern with honesty, integrity, and justice. ~~May we~~ **Help us to** work

8   with her administration for the benefit of our city ~~according to biblical teaching.~~ **in accordance with your way.** Grant this for

9   the sake of your righteous name.

Lines 2-8. Beginning with the last three words of line 2, this ceases to be a prayer to the end of line 8. Nothing is asked of God nor offered to God by way of praise or lament.

Lines 3-4. The words are directed to the assembly and contain a certain amount of information offered to those gathered. Surely God already knows that this is what Paul wrote! Furthermore, Paul is an apostle to Christians, but not to others. Even within a prayer in a Christian assembly this manner of phrasing is a bit didactic; if writing this for Christians only, I would revise the sentence to read: "In Christ you have called us to live together in harmony."

Line 4. Saying "together" and "with one another" is redundancy. Choose one. It can be argued that neither phrase is needed; "to live in harmony" implies the same interaction of human beings.

Line 8. The reference to "biblical teaching" is problematic. Both Jews and Christians refer to their Scriptures as "the Bible," even though their two canons vary in arrangement and content. Muslims revere the Testaments to an extent, but place them well below the Koran in importance. The so-called "Eastern religions" (Hinduism, Buddhism, Shintoism, Taoism, etc.) have very different sacred texts. In all cases, the safest course of action is to rephrase the purpose of this petition.

Postscript Concerning "Mixed" Occasions

A word needs to be said about situations that can be called "mixed." These have to do with occasions on which prayer is firmly inside the church and yet includes persons who are of traditions outside of the church. For example, a Sunday service of Christians may have in it visitors of other faiths. So also persons of other religious persuasions likely will attend the weddings and funerals of Christian people.

These visitors understand themselves to be guests and do not normally expect accommodations to be made to their presence, except perhaps for comments about matters that need to be explained to save them embarrassment (such as who is welcome to receive Holy Communion). Certainly such visitors hardly expect us to modify our usual practice of prayer for their benefit, any more than we would expect Muslims at prayer to delete the name of Allah or to refrain from prostrating themselves in the direction of Mecca if we happened to be visitors at a regular service at a mosque.

One exception should be noted. Roman Catholics, following the translation of the *Jerusalem Bible* (and Protestants to a lesser extent) have recently admitted into their prayers the divine name "Yahweh." To devout Jews this is a scandalous practice. For millennia the Hebrew letters rendered into English as YHWH (without vowels, according to the usual manner of Hebrew) have been unvocalized within Judaism. This title for God, given to Moses at the burning bush (Exodus 3:14), is regarded by Jews as being too holy ever to say aloud. Hence, this sacred name is never uttered in prayer; when encountered in the oral reading of Scripture, another title for God ("the LORD," in English) is substituted wherever YHWH appears in the Hebrew text. Therefore the use of "Yahweh" (or the older and inaccurate "Jehovah") should be shunned when Jews are present, even at a Sunday service of the church. Indeed, there are a number of us who as Christians believe Judaism herein has a noble insight into the majesty and mystery of God and into the reverence with which we all ought to approach the divine presence; and therefore as Christians we prefer never to utter the sacred name aloud, whether Jews are present or not. (On this point, review the early portion of exercise 10, as necessary.)

Now I want you to look at the prayer you wrote in exercise 18 for an ecumenical conference. Imagine that instead of being an assembly of all Christians, the conference is to be interfaith and that the prayer is to be written so that all present may say the amen. What in your prayer must be changed if this is to be possible? Comb carefully through your prayer for all specifically Christian references and anything else that may be troublesome to persons of other faiths. Then rewrite the prayer below for use in the interfaith gathering.

Read through your prayer to be certain it is appropriate to the setting described, and also to be sure that this edited version flows well for oral use.

Exercise 19

Writing Prayers for Unison Use

Read Jude 20-25.

In our studies of the litany and prayer of confession, we have dealt somewhat with prayers that are spoken by a group of people. Nor is unison prayer limited to those two forms. Now we look in a more concentrated way at the problems and potential of unison prayer.

Those who have had a long association with the church take unison speech for granted. For nearly half a millennium most Protestants have said the Lord's Prayer, the Creeds, and other prayers and acts of worship in unison; some of these we have memorized, but others are read from books or weekly bulletins. Therefore it may never occur to us that unison speech is very rare in our culture generally. The newcomer to the church in the United States may have never said anything in unison except the Pledge of Allegiance to the Flag; that is spoken from memory, and hence this visitor may literally never have read anything at all in unison from a printed text. In other words, what most of my readers take for granted as being comfortable may to a newcomer seem odd, awkward, even offensive.

Therefore anything written for unison reading requires great care on the author's part. Complicated grammatical constructions and strange words make unison reading difficult at best. Some challenges may be overcome if the written prayer is used on multiple occasions in close proximity; familiarity increases both ease of reading and comprehension. But a prayer written for unison use on only one occasion (or for use only once every six months or year) must be totally straightforward and simple, or it will be read badly. When those who read aloud stumble over words or get lost in multiple clauses, prayer is dissipated. Instead of being a joy, praying then becomes a chore.

My usual advice that a draft of a prayer be read aloud before being perfected now must be intensified. It is not sufficient that it be read aloud by the author (who knows all too well the words and the grammatical ins and outs). If possible, the draft should be read by at least four or five people at the same time, none of whom has seen it before. In other words, the situation that will occur within the service of worship should be anticipated before the prayer goes to print. Those who do this unison reading should be asked to comment on where and why the task seemed difficult.

In many churches, the best tactic may be to make sufficient copies of the proposed prayer to be read aloud by choir members at their weekly rehearsal. (If the bulletin must go to press before that occasion, you will need to work ten or twelve days ahead in your preparation.) Most choirs are reasonably representative of the congregation as a whole in age, education, gender, and reading ability. Trying a prayer out on the paid staff of the church (if there is one) will be less effective. The latter group is apt to be smaller and more homogeneous than the choir. Furthermore, the familiarity with the text that the choir achieves at rehearsal time will enable its members to give confident vocal leadership to the rest of the congregation when the prayer is used in the service of corporate worship.

Before beginning to write for unison speech there are certain principles to keep in mind concerning word choice and sentence structure.

As to vocabulary: All words used should be familiar and readily understood. There is a fine prayer with which I am familiar that uses the word "magnanimity." Never should that prayer be attempted in unison! What I am about to suggest will at first seem odd and complicated. But try it anyhow.

1. Count the number of words in the prayer.
2. Count the number of syllables in the prayer.

3. Divide the larger number by the smaller number. The ideal resulting figure is 1.3 to 1.4 syllables per word. The tipping point is 1.5. Beyond that, words may be too complex for unison use. Let's apply that to the prayer we continue to use as our standard, following the current ecumenical translation.

> Our Fa-ther in heav-en,
> hal-lowed be your name;
> your king-dom come,
> your will be done, on earth as in heav-en.
> Give us to-day our dai-ly bread.
> For-give us our sins, as we for-give those who sin a-gainst us.
> Save us from the time of tri-al and de-liv-er us from e-vil.
> For the king-dom, the pow-er, and the glo-ry are yours
> now and for ev-er.

In contemporary English translation, the prayer Jesus gave us as a model for our own prayer consists of 64 words that have in total 83 syllables; 83 divided by 64 reveals an average of 1.3 (actually 1.296) syllables per word. Perfect for unison use. And unless you are writing a pre-primer for young children ("See Dick and Jane. . . .") you will not get much below 1.3 in spoken English. But neither do you want to get above 1.4 or 1.5. Let's look at a prayer that is not suitable for unison use.

> E-ter-nal-ly right-eous Sov-er-eign:
> as a com-mun-i-ty of com-pas -sion and grace
> de-di-ca-ted to hu-man-i-tar-i-an ser-vice,
> we ga-ther in hu-mil-i-ty and re-spon-sive-ness to your com-mand-ments.
> Rec-ti-fy all with-in us that is a-miss.
> Re-con-cile all who suf-fer the con-se-quen-ces of a-li-en-a-tion,
> and by your re-gen-er-a-tive pow-er grac-ious-ly trans-form us,
> mak-ing us your new peo-ple of ser-vice and de-vo-tion,
> who a-wait your will and thank-ful-ly em-bo-dy your love.

This prayer contains 64 words, as does the contemporary Lord's Prayer. But now we have 125 syllables (rather than 83). Thus the average number of syllables per word is almost 2.0 (1.95)—well over our established boundary line of 1.5 syllables per word.

The difficulty of using such a prayer in unison is subtle. There are in this prayer no words that would drive most worshipers to ask for a dictionary. Not only are all of these words familiar to church people; most of the terms can be heard on radio and television, even if in differing contexts. It is easy to suppose that because we have used familiar words, therefore the prayer can easily be read aloud in unison with comprehension. The problem lies in the last two words: "with comprehension." The people will likely pronounce all words correctly; but they will be so busy negotiating the polysyllables that when the prayer is finished, the members of the congregation will have little real understanding of what they just said. Yet prayers very much like this appear again and again in church service folders with the expectation that they are well suited for public worship.

[Note to preachers and other public speakers: It is equally true that speeches and sermons are best cast in language of 1.5 syllables or fewer per word. We who speak in public typically kid ourselves into thinking that if we use only recognizable words, our listeners will understand us. Not so, if we pile polysyllables on top of polysyllables. Readers can adjust the rate of reading to accommodate long words whose aggregate meaning is unclear; listeners either follow along at the pace of the speaker or give up. Readers can re-read a passage they find confusing. Listeners have no chance to hear again a paragraph whose meaning eluded them. Hence, the first three rules of public speaking are: 1. Be clear. 2. Be clear. 3. Be clear. Those who pray in public are indeed engaging in a form of public speaking.]

As to sentence structure and length: Sentences that are long and convoluted also create a problem. Here there is no magic rule as to how many words per sentence is too many for unison reading. The prayer just examined consists of only three sentences. The middle sentence is quite brief—seven words. The opening and closing sentences are very long, and the latter is complex in its structure. They do not "read well" aloud. Even if this were a prayer spoken by a leader rather than a congregation, the last sentence would benefit from being divided as follows:

> Reconcile all who suffer the consequences of alienation.
> By your regenerative power, graciously transform us.
> Make us your new people of service and devotion,
>> that we may await your will and thankfully embody your love.

For use as a unison prayer, I would also avoid the introductory phrase "By your regenerative power." Such grammatical twisting is fine when done by a leader, and many excellent prayers include such reversed constructions in which the verb of petition is preceded by a clause: "That we may know your will and do it, send your grace upon us." "Upon the many people across the world who suffer, bestow your healing power." But in unison prayers, the congregation is more apt to grasp meaning if the construction is straightforward: "Send your grace upon us, that we may know your will and do it." "Bestow your healing power upon the many people across the world who suffer." Put the verbs of petition up front.

So is there any hope for the prayer I presented above? Probably it would be best to tear it up and begin again. But failing that, I would recast it for unison reading as follows:

Original:
Eternally righteous Sovereign:
as a community of compassion and grace
dedicated to humanitarian service,
we gather in humility and responsiveness to your commandments.
Rectify all that is amiss.
Reconcile all who suffer the consequences of alienation,
and by your regenerative power graciously transform us,
making us your new people of service and devotion,
who await your will and thankfully embody your love.

Rewritten:
Eternal God, our ruler:
You have called us to be a people of compassion.
Enable us to serve others freely,
* to dedicate ourselves to good works.*
Cause us to do your will with humble hearts.
Set right all that is amiss in our world and community.
Reconcile all who are at odds with each other.
Transform and renew us by your gracious power.
Make us a people of service and devotion,
* that we may do your will*
* and live out your love with thanksgiving.*

The revised prayer, while not necessarily strong in content and form, is far better suited for unison reading than its antecedent. The revised prayer has 84 words with 115 syllables. Thus the average number of syllables per word is reduced from 1.95 to 1.37. The original prayer had 64 words with a total of 125 syllables. The revised prayer is actually shorter by ten syllables, though it has twenty more words—largely monosyllables.

Now construct a brief prayer for unison congregational use. (Cardinal principle: All unison prayers should be as brief as possible.) Select a topic and have in mind the kind of service for which the prayer is designed.

_____

_____

_____

_____

_____

_____

_____

_____

_____

_____

_____

_____

_____

_____

_____

_____

_____

_____

_____

_____

_____

Once you have completed a draft, count the words and also the syllables. The easiest way I have found to do a syllable count is this:

1. Count the number of words in the prayer.
2. Then, ignoring all one-syllable words and the first syllable of each polysyllable word, count only second, third, and fourth (or more) syllables of words used.
3. Add this figure to the total number of words in the prayer.
4. Divide the larger number by the smaller to determine average syllables per word.

Also look carefully at the length and complexity of the sentences.

Now revise the draft, adjusting word length and sentence structure as necessary.

Before printing this prayer, review comments near the end of exercise 9 concerning the use of sense lines and of lowercase fonts.

When you have completed the second draft, ask a group of people to read it aloud in unison. Note where they have difficulty. Also, ask them which places seem rough or awkward. Revise as needed.

Exercise 20

Presiding at the Free Intercessions

Read Colossians 1:3-10.

We first confront a problem of vocabulary. The manner of prayer under consideration has many names: the prayers of the people, the prayer of the faithful, the prayer of the church, the intentions, the intercessions, and the concerns of the congregation. What is intended by all of the labels, however, is that the members of the congregation in one way or another contribute to the content of the prayers; this manner of praying is at the opposite end of the spectrum from the pastoral prayer in which one person constructs and offers the prayer. I am using as an umbrella term "free intercessions" to indicate that there is not necessarily any specified form or written text from which to work. Someone does have to preside over this portion of the service and that person will need to give thought to how this period of prayer will be organized, how it will proceed, and how it will be terminated.

Consider several possible approaches:

In one approach, the presider simply invites members of the congregation to express their prayer requests aloud. Within this approach are two options. (a) Members of the congregation are invited to offer actual prayers, though brief ones: "O God, extend your comfort to the Diaz family in their mourning." (b) Congregants instead may simply offer a prayer concern: "For the Diaz family in their mourning." Now let us look at each option in more detail.

(a) When actual prayers are solicited, there is little the presider needs to do to close off the prayer. On the other hand, there is little the presider can do to prevent a prayer from becoming lengthy and filled with information rather than petition: "O God, extend your comfort to Maria and Antonio Diaz and their children after the death of Antonio's father from cancer yesterday afternoon. The funeral will be held at St. Mary's Church in Middletown on Tuesday morning at 10 A.M., with a viewing on the evening before," and so on.

Some congregations may be willing to make a brief fixed response after each short prayer; others will regard this possibility as being "too formal." When a response is used, the people need to be instructed in its form. Thus the presider at the beginning of the period of prayer says: "After each brief prayer offered, I will say 'Let us pray to the Lord.' Then you will say in unison, 'Lord, accept our prayer.' " Sometimes the presider asks the person offering the prayer to conclude with the lead-in-line "Let us pray to the Lord." But many will either forget to do this, or will use a different set of words, thus confusing the congregation and embarrassing themselves. It is more effective for you as presider to carry out this function. If the brief prayers are apt to number in the dozens, using a fixed response may become wearisome; this can create a negative effect that outweighs the value of vocal participation by all present. As presider, you must sense when and when not to use unison responses.

At the conclusion of the short prayers, the presider may close the period with a brief petition such as, "Receive, O Lord, these prayers spoken and those uttered silently within our hearts. We trust your wisdom concerning how our petitions are to be answered. Show us how we may contribute to alleviating the needs of those for whom we pray. And grant us your peace through Jesus Christ our Savior."

(b) Alternatively, instead of soliciting actual prayers, the presider may instead ask for prayer concerns: "For the Diaz family, in their time of mourning." Many worshipers are more comfortable stating a request than forming it into an actual prayer.

As presider, you will need to acknowledge each request in some way. The best response is merely a nod of your head or a gentle "thank you" when the request is finished and it is time to move to the next person. It is tempting to say more, such as: "That is a very important concern and we need to take it quite seriously." But consider what you will say after some frivolous request (for example, "Please pray for good weather for our family picnic next Saturday" or "Pray that our team will win the ball game tomorrow"). Anything more than a cursory response likely will get you into a tight place very shortly and may cause someone to allege that you have discriminated against them by not responding as enthusiastically to their request as to others made that day.

At the conclusion of the concerns, it is the task of the presider to offer a prayer that embodies the requests. This will be more ample than the brief prayer used after option (a) above. But resist the temptation to delineate every concern. This quickly bcomes tedious, and there is the great danger that you will forget one or two requests, mispronounce some proper names, or not know what to do about a concern mumbled beyond recognition. It is best mentally to sort the concerns into categories. Then, for example, pray somewhat generally for the sick and those who minister to them; for those who mourn; for those facing perplexing decisions; for the victims of a recent earthquake, flood, or fire; for those who suffer in time of war; and for other major concerns mentioned by the congregation.

One challenge of the forms of prayer just discussed is that the extent of the requests will vary from congregation to congregation, and from week to week within the same congregation. Some congregations are shy and can hardly be coaxed into saying anything. Others are voluble and can barely be stopped in their determination to speak. Furthermore, some are focused outward and will remember to mention needs drawn from national and international news as well as church matters of denominational and ecumenical importance. Other congregations, however, are quite ingrown. They will mention only persons and causes known to them personally, and thus need to have the horizons of their concern broadened. As the presider you may feel it necessary to include in your summation prayer causes that have not been mentioned that day but that should be within the concern of the congregation.

Another challenge concerns the ability of all to hear what is being said. Unless the acoustics of the room are excellent, it may be necessary for the presider or an usher to pass around a hand-held cordless microphone. Even so, that presider will need to admonish persons to speak directly into it; if such is not available, at times the presider may need to ask that requests be spoken more loudly. Some people, however, will find in this an implied criticism of their own lack of volume and may never again dare to open their mouths during the prayer time. Care must be taken to be exceedingly gracious and tactful when presiding.

At this point I ask you to pause in your reading and to reflect for several minutes on experiences you have had in congregations that used options (a) or (b). What worked well? What seemed to cause a lack of ease among the people? What did not work at all? How could the situations have been improved? It does not matter whether you were the presider in such instances or whether someone else was. Draw as much from the experiences as you can, and then return to your reading.

An alternative way of handling the prayers that may encourage a broader scope of concern is to use a form known as "the biddings" or "the bidding prayer." The name reflects the fact that the leader bids the congregation to prayer for certain things: "I bid you to pray now for the leaders of our nation and the world." "I invite your prayers for those who are in prison and for their victims." "I also ask your prayers for the bishops and other regional leaders of our church as they face difficult decisions." After each bidding there may be a period of silence, after which the presider offers a collect related to the concern mentioned. Or the biddings may be responded to vocally from the congregation as in (a) above. Either way, the presider exercises more control over the content. This kind of prayer pattern is sometimes called "directed prayer."

Note, however, that nothing is guaranteed as to vocal response. The fact that you solicit prayers or prayer concerns for the work of the United Nations does not mean anyone will actually speak to this issue. At times you will need to be content with silence. Or suppose you ask prayers for the church's Boy Scout troop and no one says a word; then you request prayers for the church's Girl Scout troop and four people offer responses. This may mean only that several members of the congregation, made uneasy by the silence in the first instance, have resolved not to allow another category to pass without vocal response. But the notion that the parish congregation is more committed to the girls than to the boys may be difficult to dispel. Nothing is risk free!

There is an honorable tradition that dictates that intercessions should begin with the general and work toward the specific. Bid prayers first for the needs of the world, then for leaders of other nations and of the church universal; then move closer to home and ask for prayers for national needs and leaders and for leaders of your own denomination. Next invite prayers related to the local community. Finally invite prayers for individuals known to the worshiping body—the sick, those who mourn, and the like. There is a lovely theology for all of this, that we should first be concerned about others and only then about ourselves. But if you want evidence of the extent and power of sin, just try this approach. I guarantee you that when you ask for the needs of the world, someone will immediately mention Aunt Sally, who had surgery on Friday, or Heinrich Schultz, whose son died suddenly. So you do well to reverse the process. First bid prayers for the sick, the confused, and the grief-stricken; then work outward. Even so, during the prayers for national leaders someone will realize no one has mentioned Tasha Washington's loss of her job and will insert this local concern into the national category. Even in the chapel of a theological seminary this confusion of categories happens all the time, so do not be upset when it occurs.

Now again I am asking you to pause in your reading. This time I want you to envision a series of five biddings to be used the four Sundays of a month you choose. For each Sunday list five categories of concern. Every week you will need a category for "the sick and those who mourn." Plan the other four categories in such a way that across a month you have variety and breadth of content. Think of civil holidays in the month of your choice that may be the occasion for prayer (New Year's Day and Martin Luther King, Jr. Day in January; Presidents' Day in February; and so on). Also consider the order in which you will place your five topics week by week.

First Sunday

1. _____

2. _____

3. _____

4. _____

5. _____

Second Sunday

1. _____

2. _____

3. _____

4. _____

5. _____

Third Sunday

1. _____

2. _____

3. _____

4. _____

5. _____

Fourth Sunday

1. _____

2. _____

3. _____

4. _____

5. _____

When you have finished, check to see whether major categories have been forgotten. Revise as necessary.

If you have regular responsibilities in a parish for presiding at bidding prayers, it is useful to keep a running list of categories covered. Once a quarter, look over the listing. In the succeeding quarter be sure to include what may have been overlooked in the quarter just ended.

A central concern related to free intercession is the inclusion in public prayer of inappropriate and confidential matters. We have mentioned this in part in exercise 16. But as a presider you face the issue from a different angle than that of the person who frames the prayer. As a presider, how do you help the congregation to know that prayers and concerns should not be phrased in ways that seem to take sides in heated ethical debates or hotly contested elections? You are not a censor who can say, "No, we can't pray about that" when someone has expressed the concern that "the electorate will vote for the liberals" next week. In part this problem can be prevented by reminding the congregation on occasion of the importance of enabling all to say amen. But at times, it may be necessary to talk in private with someone who again and again phrases things in inappropriate ways.

Keeping confidences while at prayer is even trickier. Sometimes those in distress will explicitly say, "Please don't tell anyone about this." But at other times they may assume confidentiality about issues we regard as being quite public. A death is a public event and cannot be concealed, but the family may well not want it announced that the deceased committed suicide or died of a sexually transmitted disease. Even though we may see no reason for people to be ashamed in such instances, the privacy of the family must be respected. Some people even want a hospitalization, a job loss, or a recent marriage to be kept private.

Two bits of counsel: (1) In a situation where you are uncertain about the desire for confidentiality, do not ask "May we remember you in prayer in the weekly service?" It is very difficult to answer that negatively (especially if it is being asked by your pastor). After all, no one wants to seem to be opposed to prayer. The proper question is: "Would you like to be remembered in prayer by the congregation, or would you prefer that I pray for you only in private?" Encouraging members of the congregation to ask that question can prevent some disasters during the prayer time. (2) Teach the congregation to generalize prayers. Unless congregational prayers have been specifically requested by the couple, no one should make requests on behalf of "Rob and Emily Brauster who are having marital difficulties." Nor is it even sufficient to generalize it to a request for prayers for "my neighbors who are having marital difficulties"; that may only encourage some people to speculate about which of your neighbors are meant. The request should be "for any couples who are having marital difficulties."

Occasionally while presiding you may sense a possibility of a rumor being started and will need to ask for more specific information. Once in a seminary chapel, someone mentioned the name of a person who had just been diagnosed as having cancer. The name was the same as that of a bishop who was known, by reputation at least, to many in the room. The presider wisely asked: "Is the person for whom you request prayers a United Methodist bishop or someone else of the same name?" The answer was that this was not the bishop, and a lot of unfortunate misinformation was squelched.

In some congregations, particularly where people are reticent to speak during the service, requests for prayer are gathered in writing. A version of this practice that has very little to commend it has worshipers put slips of paper in the offering plate. Then the ushers must sort the prayer slips from the offering and convey them to the pastor who, remaining seated during the singing of a hymn, sorts through them and tries to organize them into some logical sequence before it is time to offer a pastoral prayer at the close of the hymn. A variation of this is to make available at all entrances to the worship space cards to be filled out as the worshipers arrive. These are gathered up five minutes before the service, so the pastor can do the organizing in that five minute period. This, of course, excludes all late-comers from the process. Yet another variation has this prayer given by someone other than the pastor, and this prayer leader waits until the service is in progress to collect, sort through, and organize the prayer cards.

None of these three methods helps in the least with two practical difficulties. What if you cannot read the writing on the request slip, so that the person who has made the request feels offended by being omitted? And unless you know well the culture involved, how do you pronounce a Magyar surname (which may consist of almost nothing but consonants) or one from Polynesia (which may consist of almost nothing but vowels)?

Finally, any of the forms of prayer discussed here (and elsewhere in this book) are unfortunately susceptible to engendering weariness in the congregation due to their sameness. The same people make the same requests, week after week, perhaps year after year, until tedium sets in. In the days when there were no free intercessions on Sunday morning (these being reserved for prayer meeting on Wednesday evening), pastoral prayers suffered precisely the same debilitating effect that now afflicts the intercessions. As a child I knew that a particular pastor was about half finished with his weekly prayer when he petitioned the Almighty that "all may be brought into the ark of salvation." Oh, how I yearned for that ark to have its door closed and be put out to sea! I later discovered I was not exempt from the same vice. I am amazed that my first congregation did not strangle me for including in the pastoral prayer almost every week the petition that "those who suffer may be healed in body, mind, and spirit."

The solution, insofar as there is one, is to vary the forms of prayer over time. When you sense that totally free intercessions are bogging down, try directing the prayers for a few weeks—perhaps by having silence after each bidding, followed by a collect. Then shift for a time to a comprehensive or pastoral prayer. Or write a comprehensive litany. If you fear that too much variety causes the congregation anxiety because they never know what to expect next week, vary the forms by the liturgical season: pastoral prayers throughout Advent, litanies from Christmas to Epiphany, bidding prayers with silence throughout Lent, and free intercessions for the Great Fifty Days of Easter, and so on.

Now before finishing the exercise, take some time to think about these and other forms of congregational prayer you have experienced. What are the advantages and pitfalls of each? No two presiders are alike in ability and temperament, nor should we expect them to be. After assessing your own assets and limitations when leading the intercessions, what practices do you think you can use with the most ease and grace? To which do you think you may become accustomed through experience? Which forms would you prefer not to try, at least for the time being?

When you have considered all of this, select one of the four Sundays for which you planned biddings. Write five collects, one to be used after the silence that follows each bidding.

Exercise 21

The Eucharistic Prayer

Read John 6:35-40.

We began the exercises in this book by considering a prayer of praise to God. We close these exercises by considering the most pervasive act of praise to God engaged in by the church at all times and in all places—the central prayer of the Lord's Supper. It is known by varying titles: The Anaphora (Orthodoxy), the Canon of the Mass (Roman Catholicism), the Prayer of Consecration (much of Protestantism), and the Great Thanksgiving (used ecumenically today).

In the churches just listed, the texts are carefully prescribed and passed from generation to generation with certain changes of style but an agreed upon substance. Among these churches, some require that the person presiding use the approved prayers without alteration of any kind; others allow a certain latitude and even provide for a variety of options within a standard form. If you are writing a prayer within that latitude, take care to observe carefully the form and order common to the approved prayers, even though you will be writing different words to fill the accepted framework. The prescribed unison portions should not be altered unless you want to confuse the congregation mightily (and perhaps even to incur the wrath of ecclesiastical authorities).

At the opposite end of the denominational spectrum, in some of the Free Churches of the Protestant tradition (such as many Baptist or Disciples of Christ bodies) nothing is written down or even handed on orally except in an incidental way. Those designated to preside at the Lord's Table are charged with the responsibility of creating a prayer each time the people gather to receive the bread and cup. In these churches, some who preside at the Table feel free to consult books that contain suggested prayers but that do not have denominational sanction. Others offer prayers without such consultation out of the fear that any reliance on a published work will result in praying that is unauthentic or even insincere. If you are constructing a prayer in such a context, take care to determine how much latitude is given to you. Often it is expected that the prayers will be very simple in structure and that there will be no congregational responses except a final unison amen.

In short, unless you are ordained, in most denominations you will not preside at the eucharistic prayer; but anyone, lay or clergy, can construct such a prayer in those churches that permit nonprescribed texts. If you do have occasion to write a eucharistic prayer, it is mandatory that you understand your ecclesiastical tradition and the expectations of the particular congregations within it for whose use the prayer is intended.

If you feel you will never have occasion or inclination to write a Great Thanksgiving, you are excused from doing anything further in this exercise; if ever the need to know how to write such a prayer does arise, you can return to this section for assistance.

What is described below represents a basic pattern shared at present by Roman Catholics, Anglicans, Lutherans, Methodists, Presbyterians, the United Church of Christ, and others. The unison portions are derived from work done by the International Consultation on English Texts [ICET], a set of contemporary translations of ancient texts used across the English-speaking world.

The Great Thanksgiving begins with an *Introductory Dialogue* said responsively by presider and people:

The Lord be with you.
And also with you.
Lift up your hearts.

141

We lift them up to the Lord.
Let us give thanks to the Lord our God.
It is right to give God thanks and praise.

There are slight variations from this text. Some say, "We lift them up to the Lord," and others say simply, "We lift them to the Lord." The final response can read "give God thanks," "give him thanks," or "give our thanks." Some substitute "God" for "the Lord" and "God most high" for "Lord our God." But all versions are based on texts usually attributed to Hippolytus, a Christian leader in Rome who wrote around A.D. 200.

Following the Dialogue there is a recounting of the wonderful works of God, particularly as reported in the Hebrew Scriptures. For example, mention may be made of God's creation of the world and of humans in the divine image; God's covenant made with us, against which we have rebelled; God's continuing faithfulness in the face of our sin; the call to repentance given through the prophets; and so on.

Then follow the *Sanctus and Benedictus qui venit* with one or more *Prefaces*. With some variation, the Sanctus-Benedictus qui venit is:

Holy, holy, holy Lord, God of power and might,
heaven and earth are full of your glory.
    Hosanna in the highest.
Blessed is he who comes in the name of the Lord.
    Hosanna in the highest.

For centuries, certain texts have been known in English by their opening words in Latin. *Sanctus* is simply the Latin term for "holy" and *benedictus qui venit* the corollary term for "blessed is he who comes." With reference to the phrase "blessed is he who comes," many well-meaning persons have altered this to read "blessed are they who come," on the assumption that the pronoun refers to the worshiper. It does not; it refers to Christ and alludes to words from Psalm 118:26 called out when Jesus entered Jerusalem a few days before his death (Matt. 21:9, Mark 11:9, Luke 13:35, and John 12:13). Those who prefer not to use a masculine pronoun for Christ should change the line to read: "Blessed is the One who comes."

The Sanctus-Benedictus qui venit is preceded by a *General Preface*, words which lead gracefully from the general recounting of God's deeds into the congregational response quoted above. Here is a typical General Preface:

Therefore we praise you, O God,
    along with all the company of heaven
    and your faithful people of every time and place,
        as together we sing [say]:
Holy, holy, holy Lord [and so forth].

On certain occasions the General Preface is itself preceded by a *Proper Preface*, words of praise proper to a specific occasion. Thus on Pentecost Sunday, for example, the General Preface may be preceded by words such as these:

After the ascension, you sent your Holy Spirit
    upon a band of frightened followers of Jesus,
    and formed them into Christ's holy church,
giving them gifts of boldness
    and enabling them to proclaim the Gospel to all.
Therefore we praise you [and so forth].

Following the Sanctus-Benedictus qui venit, the Great Thanksgiving includes these three components, but the order in which they occur may vary:

A. *Narrative of the Work of Christ*—This may begin with a general statement of what God has done in Christ, and/or with particular statements related to the occasion (for example, recounting the Incarnation on Christmas Day or the resurrection during Easter). Then the first Eucharist is recounted in what is commonly called the *Institution Narrative*, consisting of the direct quotation of one of the following or some composite of them:

Matthew 26:26-28 or 26:26-29
Mark 14:22-24 or 14:22-25
Luke 22:14 and 19-20, perhaps with parts verses 17-18 also
1 Corinthians 11:23-25

B. *Anamnesis*—The title is a Greek word usually translated "remembrance," but it has a sense of active participation in, not merely the recital of past events. This is a particular remembrance of the work of Jesus and of the offering of ourselves made to God. Here is an example:

We now celebrate this remembrance of our redemption,
recalling the work of our Savior,
  who lived among us and taught us,
  who offered himself up for our sin,
    conquered death,
  and poured out the Spirit upon the church.
His glorious victory we await as we offer you
  ourselves with these gifts of bread and cup.

The Anamnesis may end in a *Memorial Acclamation*, a response to be sung or said, such as:

Christ has died.
Christ is risen.
Christ will come again.
or
We remember his death.
We proclaim his resurrection.
We await his coming in glory.

C. *Epiclesis*—a prayer asking that the Holy Spirit be poured upon us and upon our eucharistic gifts, that they may be for us the body and blood of Christ, and that we may be the body of Christ in the world. (*Epiclesis* is a Greek word meaning "to call in," that is, to invoke the work of the Spirit.) In some orders, the Epiclesis precedes the Institution Narrative.

Then follow *Intercessions*. These may include short remembrances of biblical persons, of saints across the ages, and of deceased Christians we have known. Normally there will be brief petitions for the welfare of the church and its mission to the world. These may conclude with an allusion to the time when we shall all gather at the great feast of heaven.

Finally there is a *Trinitarian Doxology* such as "Through Christ, with Christ, in Christ, in the unity of the Holy Spirit, all glory and honor are yours, now and forever." This leads into the *Great Amen*, said or sung by all. Not only is the concluding doxology trinitarian, but so also is the prayer as a whole. Traditionally the Prayer is offered to the Father through the Son in the power of the Spirit. In most denominations the Lord's Prayer is prayed in unison immediately after the Great Thanksgiving.

Using the material just presented, it will be useful for you to dissect the following Great Thanksgiving into its component parts, recording these by line numbers in the spaces that follow the prayer.

1   The Lord be with you.
2   **And also with you.**
3   Lift up your hearts.
4   **We lift them up to the Lord.**

5   Let us give thanks to the Lord our God.
6   **It is right to give our thanks and praise.**

7   It is right, and a good and joyful thing,
8   always and everywhere to give thanks to you,
9   Father Almighty, creator of heaven and earth.
10   You have made from one every nation and people
11   to live on all the face of the earth.

12   And so, with your people on earth and all the company of heaven
13   we praise your name and join their unending hymn:

14   **Holy, holy, holy Lord, God of power and might,**
15   **heaven and earth are full of your glory. Hosanna in the highest.**
16   **Blessed is he who comes in the name of the Lord. Hosanna in the highest.**

17   Holy are you, and blessed is your Son Jesus Christ.
18   By the baptism of his suffering, death, and resurrection
19   you gave birth to your Church,
20   delivered us from slavery to sin and death,
21   and made with us a new covenant by water and the Spirit.
22   He commissioned us to be his witnesses to the ends of the earth
23   and to make disciples of all nations,
24   and today his family in all the world is joining at his holy table.

25   On the night in which he gave himself up for us, he took bread,
26   gave thanks to you, broke the bread, gave it to his disciples, and said:
27   "Take, eat; this is my body which is given for you.
28   Do this in remembrance of me."

29   When the supper was over he took the cup,
30   gave thanks to you, gave it to his disciples, and said:
31   Drink from this, all of you; this is my blood of the new covenant,
32   poured out for you and for many for the forgiveness of sins.
33   Do this, as often as you drink it, in remembrance of me."

34   And so, in remembrance of these your mighty acts in Jesus Christ,
35   we offer ourselves in praise and thanksgiving
36   as a holy and living sacrifice, in union with Christ's offering for us,
37   as we proclaim the mystery of faith.

38   **Christ has died; Christ is risen; Christ will come again.**

39   Pour out your Holy Spirit on us gathered here,
40   and on these gifts of bread and wine.
41   Make them be for us the body and blood of Christ,
42   that we may be for the world the body of Christ, redeemed by his blood.

43   Renew our communion with your Church throughout the world,
44   and strengthen it in every nation and among every people
45   to witness faithfully in your name.

46 By your Spirit make us one with Christ,
47   one with each other, and one in ministry to all the world,
48 until Christ comes in final victory, and we feast at his heavenly banquet.

49 Through your Son Jesus Christ, with the Holy Spirit in your holy Church,
50   all honor and glory is yours, almighty Father, now and for ever.

51 **Amen.**[14]

	Line Numbers
Introductory Dialogue	_____
Narrative of the wonderful works of God	_____
Proper Preface [optional]	_____
General Preface	_____
Sanctus and Benedictus qui venit	_____
Beginning Narrative of God's work in Christ	_____
Institution Narrative	_____
Anamnesis	_____
Memorial Acclamation	_____
Epiclesis	_____
Intercessions	_____
Concluding Doxology	_____
Great Amen	_____

(After completing your answers, check them against those found at the end of this exercise.)

Before constructing a Great Thanksgiving, it is necessary to know which parts should be used as they stand and which can be written anew. The portions designated with an asterisk are those you may wish to write if you are in a denomination that follows the set form but allows for variation in language. The portions designated "common text" are unison responses by the congregation as commonly used within your denomination. Altering these words may cause confusion in the case of spoken passages. Unless done with enormous care alteration will render passages sung to known tunes impossible to negotiate. For the Institution Narrative, use one of the New Testament narratives cited above.

Introductory Dialogue	common text
Narrative of the wonderful works of God	*
Proper Preface (optional)	*
General Preface	common text
Sanctus with Benedictus qui venit	common text
Beginning Narrative of God's work in Christ	*
Institution Narrative	from passages cited above
Anamnesis	*
Memorial Acclamation	common text
Epiclesis	*
Intercessions	*
Concluding Doxology	common text
Great Amen	common text

If you are in a denominational tradition not accustomed to this form, it may seem to you hopelessly complex and eternal in length. If you are in a tradition that takes this form for granted, you know that a well-written prayer need not be long, but can be said without rushing within three minutes (about the same amount of time it takes to sing "Amazing Grace"). But this is true only if the author of the prayer wastes not a word. Therefore the writing of a eucharistic prayer is not for the beginner. And if the unison responses of the congregation are sung, more time will be needed.

If you would like to try your hand at a eucharistic prayer, first determine which category you are in:

(a) a tradition that does not follow the pattern given above.
(b) a tradition that follows this form but allows parts of it to be written for occasional use.

If you are the first category, you will need to decide which parts of the historic form are comfortable to your people and which would seem alien. Likely the congregation will not be accustomed to an introductory dialogue or a unison memorial acclamation, for example. You may want to use a *Sanctus-Benedictus qui venit* but without having it said in unison. (These acts of praise are, after all, direct quotations from Scripture and can hardly be argued against.) The Institution Narrative is virtually mandatory in all churches, so it is simply a matter of deciding which New Testament passage to use and where it is normally placed in your tradition. (In some churches it is not a part of the prayer but is read immediately before the prayer—and then is called "the biblical warrant," for it serves as the scriptural authorization for what is to follow.) Surely no congregation can object to asking God to send the Holy Spirit upon us and upon our gifts of bread and cup, though many of these same congregations may take offense at inserting into the prayer the names of deceased Christians. Having decided what to include and exclude, write a draft of the prayer. Check it against the outline above and the choices you have made on the basis of that outline. Read it aloud to determine whether it flows well and sounds gracious. Revise as necessary.

If you are in the second category, select from among the portions marked by asterisks those parts you choose to write. (In your first attempt, at least, it is not necessary to do them all.) When your writing is completed, check what you have done against some of the published eucharistic prayers of your denomination to determine whether you are on the mark concerning content, length, and literary style. Read aloud the portions that you have written. Then read aloud the full prayer with your material properly inserted. Try to determine whether your writing style works well with the parts written by someone else. If not, in your revision work diligently to make your style match that of the parts being used with it. Get a second opinion by reading it aloud to someone else. Revise as needed.

A note to those who preside at the Eucharist: For reasons that are beyond understanding, throughout the entire English-speaking world, celebrants tend to read the words of Jesus over the bread in this fashion: "Take-eat," without any pause between the verbs. But there is no two-syllable word in English that sounds like "take-eat." Although there is no conjunction in any of the Greek texts, some contemporary denominational liturgy books have added an "and" to overcome this annoying practice. so if you have fallen into this practice and cannot break it, feel free to say "take and eat."

Correct Division of the Great Thanksgiving

	Line numbers
Introductory Dialogue	1-6
Narrative of the wonderful works of God	7-11
Proper Preface (optional)	not included
General Preface	12-13
Sanctus and Benedictus qui venit	14-16
Beginning Narrative of God's work in Christ	17-24
Institution Narrative	25-33
Anamnesis	34-37
Memorial Acclamation	38
Epiclesis	39-42
Intercessions	43-48
Concluding Doxology	49-50
Great Amen	51

In Conclusion

The formal "course" is now completed, and it has been fun having you in my "class." But as is always true of education, the real test of learning comes once you leave the classroom. If you have ever taken a year or two of a foreign language and then done no follow-up, you know well how quickly what you "learned" disappears from the old brain! Fortunately your own personal prayer life and opportunities to lead others in public prayer should provide adequate follow-up. But old habits die hard, so unless you consciously monitor the form and language of your prayers, what you have studied over a period of a few weeks or months can readily give way to patterns you may have followed for years or even decades before using this workbook.

What is the antidote to backsliding? Read again and again the prayers in the Bible, particularly the Psalms, and collections of classic prayers through the ages. And at least occasionally run down the following checklist to see how well a prayer you are preparing (or have had recorded and transcribed after the fact) measures up.

1. Examine the prayer for honesty of expression and universal appeal so that all can say the amen.
   ___Is the content true to the realities of life and the teachings of the gospel, or is it so oversimplified so that thoughtful persons cannot say the amen with integrity? Revise it until it is realistic.
   ___If used in an interreligious setting, will some present feel excluded because of references that are explicitly Christian?
   ___What persons may feel excluded on other grounds? How can you embrace their concerns?

2. If the prayer is intended to be of a specific type (prayer of pure praise, pastoral prayer, collect, confession, lament, litany), check to see that you have been true to that type.

3. Circle all the verbs in the prayer and underline all nouns. Then:
   ___Read the verbs aloud. Are they vigorous and bold?
   ___Replace anemic verbs of petition such as "be with."
   ___Can any nouns be used as verbs, so that "Give your power" becomes "Empower," or "Grant unity" becomes "Unite"?

4. Relentlessly continue editing as follows:
   ___Cull words that do no work: For example: "We pray that you would," "We want to pray for" or "We come to you asking that you might."
   ___Be certain the entire prayer is addressed to God. "May we" and "Let us" are directed to the congregation not to God. Replace these with verbs of petition. Change any occurrences of "God's love" or "God's grace" to "your love" or "your grace."
   ___Count the number of times you address the Almighty with terms such as *God, Lord, Father/Mother,* and so on. In a collect or other short prayer, there should be only one address. Even in a longer prayer, take care that you are not using addresses so often that the prayer sounds choppy or that you seem to be addressing an inattentive deity.

___Have you used the word *just* other than to refer to justice? If so, delete it.

___Have you used the word *might* other than to refer to strength? If so, change it to *may* unless it is in the past tense.

5. Check trinitarian theology.

___If the address is directed to one of the Persons of the Trinity, are the other two mentioned in the closing?

___Is there any confusion of Persons (such as, "Father, we thank you for dying on the cross")?

___If you have constructed a three-part prayer with one part addressed to each Person separately, are the parts parallel and balanced?

6. If the prayer is to be printed out in a church service folder or other publication:

___Check all spelling. Do not rely on a spell check computer feature. Likely it does not recognize the difference between *O* and *Oh*, nor between *guilt* and *gilt* or *quilt*.

___Check all grammar and punctuation.

7. If the prayer is printed out for unison reading by the congregation:

___Check word length; reduce to 1.5 syllables per word or lower.

___Check sentence length and complexity. Break long sentences down into two or three more easily understood parts.

___Be certain all of the words are known to the congregation and are easily read aloud.

___Be certain there are no tongue twisters such as, "Good Shepherd, ensure that your sheep shall be saved." (Inevitably people will be requesting that the sheep be "shaved.")

___Use sense lines rather than a margin-to-margin format.

___Employ uppercase letters only for proper nouns and at the beginning of sentences.

___Do not use a font that is difficult to read. Save the fancy fonts for other purposes.

___Ask a half dozen or more people to read the prayer aloud in your presence; if there are "rough spots," rephrase the wording until it reads smoothly.

It should be obvious that you are not going to use this checklist for every prayer each week. But every few months make yourself accountable to these principles of editing. Over time you will need to look at the checklist less and less because its content will become a part of your "internal editor." And over time not only your written prayers but your extemporaneous ones will more and more conform to these principles. Then you will be able to pray with grace and ease, even when someone who has not consulted you beforehand publicly calls out your name followed by the words "will now lead us in prayer."

Appendix 1

Selected Prayers and Their Use

This brief anthology sets forth, and in most instances adapts for contemporary use, prayers written across the ages. The books from which these prayers are taken (as found in the Notes) form a basic bibliography for those who wish to consult collections of prayers. The materials are set out here in sense lines, although they are printed margin-to margin in almost every case in the books cited. In those instances where these prayers can be used today, sixteenth- and seventeenth-century phraseology has been replaced with current usage. These and other slight alterations of style have in no way altered basic content.

Pure Praise

Saint Catherine of Siena wrote this prayer of pure praise in the fourteenth century.

Dear Lord,
    it seems that you are so madly in love with your creatures
        that you could not live without us.
So you created us;
    and then, when we turned away from you, you redeemed us.
Yet you are God, and so have no need of us.
Your greatness is made no greater by our creation;
your power is made no stronger by our redemption.
You have no duty to care for us,
    no debt to re-pay us.
It is love, and love alone, which moves you.[15]

Collects

The antiquity of the collect is evidenced by this prayer for use before the public reading of scripture and the sermon, written by Ambrose (340–397), Bishop of Milan.

O God Almighty,
you cleansed the lips of the prophet Isaiah with a burning coal.
Cleanse my heart and my lips by your favor and mercy,
that I may be able to proclaim worthily your holy Gospel;
through Jesus Christ our Lord.[16]

From Kenya comes a twentieth-century collect written by Naftali Okello Siwa. Notice that there is a double attribution: "you sent . . ." and "your Son in turn sent . . ."

Eternal Father,
you sent your Son to bring the Good News of your forgiving love
    to us sinners. Your Son in turn sent the Holy Spirit to continue
    his mission on earth through the Church.
Quicken us, we pray, by the same Spirit
that we shall not rest until all people are reached with your Gospel,
through Jesus Christ our Lord. [17]

Prayers with Vigorous Verbs

This prayer from the Masai people of Tanzania is a model of both vigorous verbs and unity of subject:

For your blessing, we thank you, God: faith in you.
Increase it, we beg, so that we no longer doubt.
Drive out all our miserliness, so that we do not refuse you anything.
Increase our faith, for the sake of those without faith.
Make us instruments of your faith, for those with only a little.
Fill our bodies with faith, our bodies that work for you all our days.
Help us to avoid the enemies of our faith, or to overcome them.
You are with us in confrontations; this we believe.
In your hands we place ourselves, and are secure.
Make haste to enter our hearts; make haste.[18]

A classic from the American Social Gospel movement is this prayer for the church by Walter Rauschenbusch. Note the verbs of petition in the second half of the prayer.

O God,
we pray for your Church,
    which is set today amid the perplexities of a changing order,
    and face to face with a great new task.
We remember with love
    the nurture she gave to our spiritual life in its infancy,
    the tasks she set for our growing strength,
    the influence of the devoted hearts she gathers,
    the steadfast power for good she has exerted.
When we compare her with all human institutions,
    we rejoice, for there is none like her.
But when we judge her by the mind of the Master,
    we bow in pity and contrition.

Oh, baptize her afresh in the life-giving spirit of Jesus!
Grant her a new birth,
    though it be with the travail of repentance and humiliation.
Bestow upon her
    a more imperious responsiveness to duty,
    a swifter compassion with suffering,
    and an utter loyalty to the will of God.
Put upon her lips the ancient Gospel of her Lord.
Help her to proclaim boldly the coming of the kingdom of God
    and the doom of all that resist it.
Fill her with the prophets' scorn of tyranny,
    and with a Christ-like tenderness for the heavy-laden and down-trodden.

Give her faith
>to espouse the cause of the people, and
>in their hands that grope after freedom and light
>to recognize the bleeding hands of Christ.

Bid her cease from seeking her own life, lest she lose it.
Make her valiant to give up her life to humanity,
>that like her crucified Lord,
>>she may mount by the path of the Cross to a higher glory. [19]

Models of Brevity

From the medieval mystic, Hildegaard of Bingen:

Beautiful God:
>Strip from me this ugly, dirty coat of sin,
>and put on me the bright, pure garment of the Spirit.

Brave God:
>Drive from me the growling wolves of corruption
>>that threaten to attack me,
>and bring to my side your gentle Lamb who can always protect me.[20]

Saint Sarrah of Libya wrote this brief prayer in the fourth century, intending it for personal use at the sixth hour of the day. Her prayer consists of two attributions followed by three petitions and a brief ascription. It alludes to three passages of scripture. Note its simplicity and elegance.

O Lord,
you who have measured
the heights and the earth
in the hollow of your hand,   [Isaiah 40:12]
and created the six-wing Seraphim
to cry out to you with an unceasing voice
Holy, Holy, Holy,   [Isaiah 6:3]
glory to your name.
Deliver me
from the mouth of the evil one, O Master.   [Psalm 22:21]
Forget my many evil deeds
and through the multitude of your compassions
grant me daily forgiveness,
for you are blessed unto the ages.[21]

Lament

Laments are less "transportable" than many other prayers because they are related to a very specific set of circumstances that likely differ from those of other experiences. This lament grew out of the experience of slavery and its aftermath in the United States. The traditional language forms are retained here, inasmuch as this prayer is less likely to be used now without the significant alteration needed to lament the effects of discrimination and racism in our own time.

In 1831, Maria W. Stewart, an African American author and leader, published a prayer from which the following is excerpted. Like many biblical laments, it ends with positive petition and praise.

O Lord God,
the sentries of Zion have called peace, peace, when there was no peace;
they have been, as it were, blind leaders of the blind.
Wherefore hast thou so long withheld from us
    the influence of thy Holy Spirit?
Wherefore hast thou hardened our hearts and blinded our eyes?
It is because we have honored thee with our lips,
    when our hearts were far from thee.

Return again unto us, O Lord God, we beseech thee,
    and pardon the iniquity of thy servants.
Cause thy face to shine upon us, and we shall be saved.
O visit us with thy salvation.
Raise up sons and daughters unto Abraham,
    and grant that there may be a mighty shaking of dry bones among us,
        a great ingathering of souls.
Quicken thy professing children.
Grant that the young may be constrained to believe
    that there is reality in religion,
    and a beauty in the fear of the Lord.
Be pleased to grant
    that the kingdom of the Lord Jesus Christ may be built up,
    that all nations and kindreds and tongues and peoples may be
        brought to the knowledge of the truth as it is in Jesus,
    and we meet around thy throne,
        and join in celebrating thy praises.[22]

A Prayer Based on Scripture

This prayer of pure praise from Africa is drawn from Ephesians 1:3-18.

All glorious God, we give you thanks:
in your Son Jesus Christ you have given us every
   spiritual blessing in the heavenly realms.
You chose us, before the world was made,
   to be your holy people, without fault in your sight.
You adopted us as your children in Christ.
You have set us free by his blood,
   you have forgiven our sin.
You have made known to us your secret purpose, to
   bring heaven and earth into unity in Christ.
You have given us your Holy Spirit,
   the seal and pledge of our inheritance.

All praise and glory be yours, O God,
   for the richness of your grace,
   for the splendor of your gifts,
   for the wonder of your love.[23]

Prayers for Particular Occasions

Slightly adapted from the original published in 1929, is this prayer for a couple on their wedding day. It was written by Lewis Garnett Jordan, a leader of the National Baptist Convention.

Our Father in heaven:
You have, in your wise and tender care for humanity,
   ordained and blessed the institution of matrimony.
Now graciously regard your servant and handmaiden
   who have solemnly pledged themselves to each other
   and have sworn unto you.
Grant that, through your good care and guidance:
   They may evermore remember and keep these vows;
   they may be kept themselves in unbroken concord and sympathy
     all the days of their earthly life,
   and may be at last, with all those near and most dear unto them,
   gathered an unbroken household to your right hand on the day of judgment.
And grant that all of us assembled here may be part of that blessed company
   who shall be called to go into the Marriage Supper of the Lamb.
This we ask only in the name and through the merits of him,
   your own Son and our Redeemer, the Lord Jesus Christ.[24]

Adapted from a somewhat longer prayer by Georgia Harkness, the first woman to hold a chair in systematic theology at a major seminary, this prayer to be used by those who are ill is very commendable for three reasons. (1) It is thoroughly honest and realistic, admitting openly that some illness will result in death. (2) It is cast in language that is plural yet quite personal, whereas most prayer by the ill is very individualistic. (3) It is filled with trust and hope in the midst of distress. It is an ideal prayer for a healing service or for a worship service in a hospital chapel.

O God,
   you forgive our iniquities and heal our diseases.
We cry to you.
Our strength has been brought low,
   and we know not what the future holds.
In our bodies, there is pain;
   in our souls, anxiety and unrest.

If it may be, restore us to health.
We ask no miracle of deliverance,
   and if in the order of nature our suffering must continue,
      help us to accept it without rebellion.
If it must lead toward the valley of the shadow,
      help us to fear no evil,
   but to go forward bravely into your nearer presence.

   In your good keeping, all is well.
   Into your hands we commend our bodies and our spirits.
Do with us as you will.[25]

Personal Prayer Favorites

Personal Prayer Favorites

Appendix 2

Praying in "The King James Way"

We deal here with three questions that may be of great concern to some who use this book and of no concern at all to the rest (which is why this is in an appendix).

1. How is it we came to address God in the now strange language of "thee" and "thou" and "wouldest" and "shouldest"?
2. What are the reasons, good and not so good, for continuing this usage in public prayer?
3. For those who wish to continue the use but have forgotten the old grammar, what are some basic rules?

How Did "Traditional" Language Come to Us?

The answer to the first question requires a brief history lesson. Prior to the middle of the twentieth century, English-speaking Christians across the world retained the language of prayer inherited primarily through the books of Common Prayer and the 1611 Authorized Version of the Bible. In constructing the 1549 and 1552 editions of the prayer book, Thomas Cranmer, Archbishop of Canterbury, depended heavily on the language of Miles Coverdale, who translated the Scriptures into English in 1535 and edited the Great Bible of 1539. In the popular mind, however, the "old way" of praying is associated less with Coverdale and Cranmer than with King James I of England because he was the patron of the 1611 translation of the Bible, and for 350 years that Authorized Version dominated Protestant piety.

Even English-speaking Roman Catholics and Orthodox Christians adopted traditional styles of language, though they rejected both the Protestant prayer books and the 1611 translation of the Scriptures. Until after Vatican II, for liturgical purposes Catholics used Latin texts; but when these were translated for the convenience of those who did not understand Latin, the translations sounded remarkably like Coverdale, Cranmer, and the Authorized Version grammarians. So also do bilingual versions of various Orthodox liturgies currently in use.

When the Second Vatican Council moved the Roman Catholic liturgy from Latin to vernacular usage in the 1960s, their English-speaking revisers deemed it well to forgo the archaic forms in favor of the style of English used in daily discourse. Protestant revisers of Scripture and worship materials quickly followed suit, and except for retaining traditionally worded hymnody and the Lord's Prayer as they learned it in childhood, many Protestant congregations soon became quite comfortable addressing God as "you." Many congregations, but not all. Even four decades later, some Protestant congregations resist the use of contemporary English while at prayer. Therefore, it is helpful to separate good reasons for retaining traditional language from reasons that are less defensible.

Should We Use the "Traditional" Forms Today?

The traditional forms are now used primarily when leading a congregation that feels ill-at-ease addressing God in conversational English. This includes congregations that retain the use of the Authorized Version of Scripture exclusively (or almost so) and to a large extent understand its vocabulary. Such congregations perhaps also make little use of recent hymn texts or other forms of liturgy that address God as "you." Indeed, the context of prayers in the traditional mode may be services such as Rite I liturgies in the Episcopal *Book of Common Prayer*, and Eucharistic Prayer IV of United Methodism's Word and Table rites.

So what are the reasons, good or not so good, for retaining the old usages? A strong preference for traditional language is to be respected but should not be defended or advocated for reasons other than that of familiarity due to habit. Therefore several inadequate or questionable reasons for retaining traditional language need to be addressed.

1. Of the defenses that do not stand up well, the strongest is that the King James style language is elegant, poetic, even majestic—that it has to it a cadence lacking in modern translations. Whether this is true or not is beside the point. The point is that in most congregations this appeal applies to a minority of persons, while the majority of worshipers are hampered from a full appropriation of the language by words and grammatical forms they no longer comprehend. We must weigh carefully the reaction of the worshipers who say, "It certainly sounds pretty, but I often am unclear about what it means."

2. Incredible as it may seem, some people appear to believe that *thee* and *thou* and *wouldest* and *shouldest* are the language forms of Jesus and the apostles. This notion would be laughable were it not accepted with such great piety by some. Jesus and all of those around him spoke to God as they spoke to one another, in the conversational forms of their day. They had no other options in their linguistic systems. There were no special forms of pronouns or verbs used for addressing God in prayer in the Hebrew, Aramaic, or Greek tongues. The English forms we have inherited have been used in worship for fewer than five hundred years; they have no biblical basis.

3. Some languages have developed forms of address that are reserved for persons of great dignity or for strangers. In German, for example, a family member or a friend is addressed as *du* (you), and this is known as "the familiar form of address." But someone you have just met or a dignitary is addressed as *Sie*, which is actually the plural form of *du*, the same word with which a group of people well known to you would be addressed. This is known as "the polite form of address." It might be supposed that the great dignity of God would compel German worshipers to address the Almighty as *Sie*. But beginning with Luther's translation of the Bible, God has been addressed by German-speaking Christians as *du*, that is, as a parent or close friend. The Scriptures provide ample permission, even encouragement, for regarding God as both.

In the history of the English language (which is closely related to German) some parallel developments occurred but have not endured. In the days when the first Protestant prayers were written in England and the earliest translations of Scripture made, both familiar and polite forms of address were used. A member of the family or a friend was addressed as *thou*, the accepted singular form of the pronoun. Strangers and dignitaries were given the honor of being called by the plural form, or the polite form of the second person, *you*. At some point as a person moved from being a stranger to being a friend, a shift from *you* to *thou* occurred. Over time, however, it became fashionable to address more and more people in the plural *you* as a kind of exaggerated courtesy, until finally the familiar forms disappeared from conversational speech, and everyone who had once been a *thou* instead became a *you*. This is a great loss to the English language, and it is a pity that the corrective found in the *y'all* of the American South has never come to be regarded as a standard English form that enables us to distinguish between second-person singular and plural.

A notable exception to the disappearance of separate second-person singular and plural forms occurred among the people commonly called Quakers. Because their official name is "The Religious Society of Friends," and because they greatly disliked pretense and social stratification, they objected to the practice of addressing everyone in the plural (the old way of addressing royalty in England). They insisted on speaking to each other in the familiar address— as friends. Today many members of the Society use conventional English when addressing non-Friends, but still use *thee* in the inner circle as an indication of their "friendliness." At the Quaker college I attended in the days when phone calls were still handled by people rather than computers, the elderly switchboard operator would always respond to a number given to her with the words, "Thank thee." Particularly to those of us who were not Quakers, it seemed quaint, even distant. But Amy intended it to be an intimate form of address; for even the greenest college student or the atheistic professor of philosophy was in her understanding a friend, to be greeted as one would greet Christ.

And that is the point. We are the friends of God (John 15:14-15). Traditional language cannot be defended under the argument that by using archaic forms we exalt the holiness of a God who is too majestic to be spoken to in ordinary ways. *Thee* and *thou* originally conveyed a sense of closeness, but history has played tricks on us and now these seem to convey distance. God is indeed distant in the sense of being holy and majestic. But the mystery of faith is this: That when we are at prayer, the holy God is closer to us than any human being can be, and thus is addressed reverently and yet in the most familiar way we know. In any setting in which the use of traditional forms makes praying seem odd or distant, those forms should be abandoned as being inimical to the very nature of Christian prayer.

Retaining King James style language cannot be defended on the basis of supposed biblical precedent. Nor does such language by its distinctiveness suggest that God should be approached in some special manner, with language patterns that are strange to daily conversation and that keep God "at a distance" through the use of a vocabulary reserved for prayer. Even an appeal to literary "quality," while it may justify personal practices of prayer when alone, fails as a rationale when praying together. Retention of traditional language is a matter of preference that grows out of and is reinforced by habit. That does not make it either good or bad, but it does mean that congregations must weight personal familiarity and preference against other factors when debating whether to retain the old forms or move to current forms.

One matter should be central when considering whether or not to use the traditional forms of prayer, and the matter is best approached anecdotally. I grew up in a small town whose population was largely German in extraction. Those of my grandparents' generation often preferred to converse with each other in the German language they or their parents had brought across the Atlantic. My parents' generation by and large could understand German when they heard it, but were not familiar enough with its vocabulary or rules of grammar to speak it. My generation could neither understand nor speak German.

In today's church, a few people are in the situation of the first generation: They know the old forms of verbs and pronouns and can reproduce them with ease and comfort. But many more parishioners are of the second generation; they have no difficulty comprehending what is meant by *thee, thou, thy,* and *thine* or *wouldest* and *shouldest;* but they are so unsure about which of these to use that they are terror stricken by the thought of having to pray publicly in this idiom. ("Is this the time to use *thee* or *thou?* Is it *wouldst* or *wouldest* that is correct? Should I say *doth, dost, doeth,* or *doest?* I will be so embarrassed if I use the wrong word!") And the upcoming generation may not even know the meaning of the words, particularly more obscure traditional terms such as *vouchsafe* and *deign.* (One wonders what brides and grooms suppose they are promising if they are required to say to one another, "And thereto I plight thee my troth"!)

Given this situation, any decision by a congregation to use the older forms exclusively has two drawbacks that need to be considered carefully:

1. The exclusive use of traditional forms of prayer may well discourage prayer among the "middle generation" and certainly will have this effect on the third generation. It will deter such people from praying aloud in the presence of others. But it will less obviously also discourage them from addressing God even in private, if they believe only archaic usage is appropriate in the presence of the Almighty. Public prayer is generally the most effective tutor for private prayer. If what is done in public is perceived as odd or even alien, private prayer will decline and perhaps even disappear in the daily lives of Christians.
2. The use (even if not exclusive) of the traditional forms can therefore be a significant impediment to evangelism. People who have never been exposed to the life of the church are not likely to want to join a group of people who "talk funny."

Of necessity, the church "talks funny" when it speaks about a God willing to go to a cross, a God who then overcomes death in ways we can never begin to comprehend. The essence of the gospel message cannot be compromised to attract the uninitiated. Indeed, if we believe the gospel at all, we will surely have some conviction that it is precisely this strange message of divine humiliation and transformation that people must have to make sense of life. But if the necessarily strange content of the gospel cannot be jettisoned, why complicate evangelism by insisting also on a strange grammatical expression that is not of the essence at all, and sometimes is at cross purposes with it? At a minimum, the strangeness of the faith should be presented in English that is straightforward.

Often compromises ensue as congregations wrestle with language issues. It may be decided, for example, that in any given service there will be at least one prayer in each language style. Or a congregation will keep the traditional forms in hymns and familiar prayers, but turn to current forms of prayers devised particularly for each occasion. Such "mixed usage" can be tolerated quite well in most instances. What is more difficult to bear is a sloppy switching between styles within the same prayer. For anyone even slightly attuned to the sounds of English prayer, it can be very distracting to attempt to follow in prayer a leader who proceeds in this manner:

God of the ages, thou hast set us on our course in life; for you offer us the gift of your presence. We are surrounded on every hand by thy mercy. Your name is to be praised throughout the earth and by all its peoples, for thou art worthy of our adoration. . . .

At the onset of offering a public prayer, a decision about style of language should be made and then adhered to until the end. (This is less important in private prayer; for we can assume that God is undistracted by such inconsistency and looks upon our intentions rather than our grammatical clumsiness.)

Policy decisions about language style should be worked through slowly and deliberately in the life of a congregation. Until this is done, the leader of prayer may need to use the traditional language where that is expected by those who are being led, and will wish to use it with sufficient accuracy and grace as to advance rather than impede the participation of those present. But the persistent use of the sixteenth- and seventeenth-century language forms while at prayer will prevail only in those congregations that insist on the use of the 1611 Bible or some slight alteration thereof. Congregations that are comfortable with contemporary translations of the Scriptures sooner or later will become very uncomfortable with prayer language that is not equally contemporary.

What Are the Basic Rules of the Old Grammar?

Having tried my best to talk you out of praying in "the King James way," for the sake of those persons who are not persuaded or who are implored by their congregations to use archaic forms, I turn now to the third question, concerning basic rules. The traditional language of English prayer differs from current language in two major ways:

1. Pronouns in the second person singular
2. Certain verbs in the second and third person singular

1. Pronouns in the second person singular

Second person singular refers to one person being addressed: *you* and its variant forms. Second person plural—*you* referring to more than one person [*y'all*]— is not affected. Because in prayer we are addressing God (the Eternal *You*), careful attention needs to be given to pronoun usage.

Here are the corresponding current and traditional forms, with each illustrated in a sentence.

You becomes *thou* when used as the subject of the sentence:
    You are worthy.
Thou art worthy. (We will deal with the verb shift from *are* to *art* later.)
You becomes *thee* when used as an object:

Direct object of the verb -	We praise *you*.
	We praise *thee*.
Indirect object of the verb -	We give *you* praise.
	We give *thee* praise.
Object of a preposition -	We give praise to *you*.
	We give praise to *thee*.

Your becomes *thy* when preceding a consonant sound:
    Your kingdom come.
    Thy kingdom come.
Your becomes *thine* when preceding a vowel sound:
    Your angels shall rejoice.
    Thine angels shall rejoice.
Yours always becomes *thine*:
    Yours is the kingdom and the power.
    Thine is the kingdom and the power.

In summary, when moving from conversational language to the older forms:

You	becomes	*thou* or *thee*, depending on whether it is the subject or an object.
Your	becomes	*thy* or *thine*, depending on whether if precedes a consonant or vowel sound.
Yours	becomes	*thine*.

Remember that all of this applies only in the singular. In the plural there are no changes with one exception: When it acts as the subject of a clause, the second person plural (*you* in the sense of *y'all*) is rendered *ye*, as in "Ye that do truly and earnestly repent of your sins." Since God, even as Trinity, is addressed in the second person singular, and since those who are being led in prayer are never addressed directly by the leader while at prayer, there is almost no occasion to use *ye* in prayer. An exception occurs if the prayer includes a direct quotation from scripture in which a group of people are being addressed, thus:

Holy God, through the prophet Isaiah thou hast given the instruction, "Comfort ye my people." Therefore we seek thy wisdom and strength, that we may be of comfort to others. . . .

But the more usual form would be an allusion to the biblical passage rather than its direct quotation, as follows, Holy God, through the prophet Isaiah thou hast instructed us to comfort thy people. Therefore, we seek. . . .

Hence most leaders of prayer do not need to worry about the use of *ye*.
Now for the more complicated matter of verbs.

2. Verbs
Verbs are altered in two instances:
Second person singular verbs commonly take an *-est* ending (or *-st* if the word ends in *e*.)

> You *come* and *go* forth in peace.
> Thou *comest* and *goest* forth in peace.

Third person singular verbs, commonly take an *-eth* (or *-th*) ending; but the *s* that ends such English verbs is first dropped. (Third person refers to *she/he/it*.)

> Time *makes* all things plain.
> Time *maketh* all things plain.
> The wise person *acts* carefully.
> The wise person *acteth* carefully.

Some very common forms are in effect contractions. For example, the second person singular form of *are* is *art*, not *arest* as the rule above would seem to suggest. *Has* becomes *hast*, not *hasest*, and *will* and *shall* becomes *wilt* and *shalt*.

Note that first person singular verbs (having to do with *I*) do not change at all, nor do plural verbs change (those that refer to "*we, you [y'all]*, or *they*.) Here are some forms frequently used in prayer that do change:

	Current forms		**Traditional forms**	
	2nd person	*3rd person*	*2nd person*	*3rd person*
Common main forms	you give	it gives	thou givest	it giveth
	you make	it makes	thou makest	it maketh
	you see	it sees	thou seest	it seeth
	you walk	it walks	thou walkest	it walketh
	you want	it wants	thou wantest	it wanteth
Common auxiliary forms ("helping verbs")				
	you are	it is	thou art	it is*
	you do	it does	thou dost**	it doth**
	you have	it has	thou hast	it hath
	you shall	it shall	thou shalt	it shall*

you should	it should	thou shouldest	it should*
you will	it will	thou wilt	it will*
you would	it would	thou wouldest	it would*

*Note that some common auxiliary verbs do not change in the 3rd person singular.

**As an auxiliary *do* becomes *dost* or *doth*. But when it stands alone as a verb, it becomes *doest* or *doeth*.

Examples:

> Holy God, thy love *dost endure* forever.
> Holy God, thou *doest* all things according to thy will.
> Blessed is the one who *doth serve* the Lord.
> Blessed is the one who *doeth* what is right.

In compound verbs (*has made, had done,*) it is only the auxiliary verb that changes, not the main verb. Therefore "You *have made* all things" becomes "Thou *hast made* all things" not "Thou hast madest all things." "You who had done all things . . ." becomes "Thou who *hadst done* all things. . . ." If the auxiliary is a verb that does not change, nothing is altered; in both King James and contemporary English the correct third person form is "The faithful person *will keep* your [thy] commandments, O Lord." (Just to confuse you, the second person form does change: "Thou *wilt keep* us in safety, O Lord.")

There are no changes in the future tense having a third person subject. "God will make all things plain" undergoes no alteration when moving from current to traditional forms. "God will maketh things plain some day" and "God willeth make things plain some day" are both bad form. However, it is correct to say, "O God [second person], thou willest not the death of sinners" and "God [third person] willeth not the death of sinners" because in these two instances *will* is a present tense verb referring to the will of God; it is not a future tense acting as an auxiliary to a main verb (*make*, in this case).

Thus far we have been dealing with indicative verbs. Note especially that the verbs *do not change at all* in the imperative. "Send forth your Holy Spirit" does not become "Sendest forth thy Holy Spirit." "Grant us your peace" does not become "Grantest us thy peace." This is an important rule to master, since prayer of petition is usually addressed to God in the imperative form.

Therefore it follows that the easiest prayers to write in the King James styles are intercessions. Within such prayers of petition there may be one or two attributions that use indicative verbs, but the vast majority of verbs in the second person are imperative (with an implied you as their subject). Contrariwise, the most difficult form of prayer to cast in the old forms is that of pure praise; for there almost everything is attribution and no requests are included.

If you wish to learn to pray in the King James way, begin by revising a collect you have written in contemporary idiom so that it conforms to the older language style. Pronouns that require alteration may be found in various sections of this prayer form; but the verbs that require change will occur primarily in the attributions (and in the closing, particularly if it is in a trinitarian form).

If you are personally unfamiliar with the traditional language but are called upon to lead in prayer a congregation that expects such forms to be used, writing out the full prayer and showing it to someone familiar with the old style is strongly recommended. Over time, you will become confident enough to be your own editor; and you may even attain the ability to pray extempore using the archaic forms. But that will not happen suddenly. Trying to figure it out on your own ahead of time or attempting to "wing it" on the spot will only increase your anxiety; that in turn can lead to more errors and confusion than would ordinarily be the case.

Reading slowly and aloud the traditional prayer books and the Authorized Version of the Bible will greatly enhance your facility at using the older forms. This is in fact how generations of Christians learned the old forms—by reading and hearing them. When I began my pastoral ministry in 1957, all public prayer was cast in those forms; yet no one ever taught us the rules of grammar necessary for correct usage. We simply "got it by osmosis," because we had heard it from earliest childhood—just as youngsters learn modern English without the aid of a grammar book. I have never seen the rules of the old grammar set forth in print. To write this appendix I have had to derive them for myself. I hope I have gotten them down correctly. If I have not, may dear Tom Cranmer, old King James, and all their retinue forgive me!

Appendix 3

Some Finer Points of Usage

For the sake of those who may wish to publish prayers, I now turn to a picayune matter. It has to do with *who* clauses, such as the attribution in a collect. Typical is the type of prayer that begins "O God, who . . ." That seems innocent enough, but immediately a booby-trap presents itself. Let's continue the sentence: "O God, who sends rain on both the just and the unjust. . . ." Perfectly straightforward and unassailably biblical, eh? Biblical yes, but hardly straightforward grammatically.

Recall that in prayer we are always addressing God in the second person—as a *you*. But the verb that goes with *you* is *send*. It would seem that only someone very careless of English would say "O God, who send . . ." Yet because we address God directly and personally "O God, who send" is absolutely correct in terms of grammar, because there is an implied but unheard *you* between *God* and *who*. But try saying it that way in public and at least 99 percent of the people you are leading in prayer will swear you have just committed a grammatical error of the first order; even second graders know better! Technically, by saying "O God, who sends . . ." we begin to talk *about* God immediately after having addressed God—which lands us directly in the "absent deity syndrome." But then as soon as the attribution is finished, we do back to talking to God.

The difficulty can be resolved by making the implied but unspoken *you* into a spoken *you*:

O God, you who send the rain on both the just and the unjust. . . .

But when the prayer is uttered aloud, it too easily sounds like this:

O God, yoo-hoo! Send the rain on both the just and the unjust.

One can also settle the matter better by saying:

O God, you are the one who sends the rain on both the just and the unjust.

But particularly in anything as terse as a collect "are the one who" is essentially useless. Therefore the best solution is this:

O God, you send the rain on both the just and the unjust.

In addition to clarifying grammatical errors that irritate teachers, journalists, and others who know their rules well, all of this explains a phenomenon you may be aware of. Until thirty years ago it was said without qualification that "A collect is a prayer consisting of one and only one sentence." But nowadays many collects in fact consist of two sentences. In shifting from "O God, who sendest" to modern speech, it is simplest to abolish the dependent relative clause beginning with *who* and to substitute an independent clause beginning with *you*. The independent clause requires a period at its end. And thereby the one sentence collect becomes two sentences: (1) address and attribution; (2) petition, purpose, and closing.

At the end of exercise 3, I gave you the commonest punctuation sequence for a collect:

Address followed by a	comma	
Attribution followed by a	period	[sometimes by a colon]
Petition followed by a	comma	
Purpose followed by a	semicolon	[sometimes by a comma]
Closing followed by a	period	

That sequence applies to contemporary collects in which the *who* clause is not used. When there is a *who* clause, it is followed by a colon; this allows the collect to consist of "one and only one sentence." Of course prayers of many kinds, not just collects, have attributive clauses related to the God whom we address.

The knowledge of all this grammatical trivia will not save the world. I warned you that it is picayune. But many copy editors tend not to be aware of this nicety in prayers, so if you send incorrect copy off to a publisher and the error is not caught, your face may be red when a reviewer accuses you of bad grammar!

Notes

1. *Book of Common Worship* (Louisville: Westminster/John Knox Press, 1993), p. 369 [joint Presbyterian].
2. *Lutheran Book of Worship* (Minneapolis: Augsburg Publishing House; and Philadelphia: Board of Publications, Lutheran Church in America, 1978), p. 29 [Collect for the Twenty-Sixth Sunday after Pentecost].
3. *Lutheran Book of Worship*, p. 25 [Collect for the ninth Sunday after Pentecost].
4. *Book of Common Prayer* (New York: The Church Hymnal Corporation and Seabury Press, 1997), p. 220 [Episcopal Collect for Wednesday in Holy Week].
5. *Book of Common Prayer*, p. 228 [Collect for the Sunday Closest to May 11].
6. "Jesus, We Look to Thee," *The Book of Hymns* (Nashville: The Methodist Publishing House, 1964), no. 310, stanzas 1 and 4.
7. Cited in John W. Doberstein's *Minister's Prayer Book* (Philadelphia: Fortress Press, n.d.), pp. 392-93, there referenced to Arthur John Gossip's *In the Secret Place of the Most High* (New York: Scribner's, 1947), p. 155-56. Reformatted for this volume, using contemporary English forms and punctuation.
8. These litanies, by the author of this book, appeared in *Liturgy*, a publication of The Liturgical Conference, respectively in Vol. 13, No. 3, pp. 1-3 and Vol. 14, No. 2, pp. iv-3.
9. *The United Methodist Hymnal* (Nashville: The United Methodist Publishing House, 1989), p. 481.
10. Robert Van de Weyer, compiler. *The HarperCollins Book of Prayers* (Edison, N.J.: Castle Books, 1997), p. 137.
11. Ronald J. Allen, ed., *Patterns of Preaching: A Sermon Sampler* (St. Louis: Chalice Press, 1998), p. 33, from Craddock's sermon entitled "Teach Us to Pray."
12. Kathy Black, *Worship Across Cultures: A Handbook* (Nashville: Abingdon Press, 1997).
13. Walter Cronkite, *A Reporter's Life* (New York: Alfred A. Knopf, 1996), pp. 219-20.
14. "Great Thanksgiving for World Communion Sunday," *The United Methodist Book of Worship* (Nashville: United Methodist Publishing House, 1992), pp. 72-73.
15. Van de Weyer, p. 90.
16. F. Forrester Church and Terrence J. Mulry, eds., *The Macmillan Book of Earliest Christian Prayers* (New York: Macmillan Publishing Co.; London: Collier Macmillan Publishers, 1988), p. 107, revised for contemporary use.
17. *Prayers Encircling the World: An International Anthology* (Louisville: Westminster John Knox Press, 1998), p. 69.
18. Desmond Tutu, ed., *An African Prayer Book* (New York et al: Doubleday, 1995), pp. 93-94.
19. Walter Rauschenbusch, *Prayers of Social Awakening* (Boston: Pilgrim Press).
20. Van de Weyer, p. 196. Reformatted.
21. Nikolaos S. Hatzinikolaou, ed. and trans. *In the Wilderness: An Anthology of Patristic Prayers* (Brookline, Mass.: Holy Cross Orthodox Press, 1988), p. 37.
22. Dorothy Porter, ed., *Early Negro Writing, 1760–1837* (Boston: Beacon Press, 1971), pp. 464-65.
23. Desmond Tutu, ed., *An African Prayer Book*, p. 69. Tutu provides no indication as to the writer of this prayer, so perhaps it is his own.
24. L. G. Gordon, *The Baptist Standard Church Directory and Busy Pastor's Guide* (Nashville: Sunday School Publishing Board of the National Baptist Convention, U.S.A., 1929), p. 101.
25. Georgia Harkness, *The Glory of God: Poems and Prayers for Devotional Use* (New York and Nashville: Abingdon-Cokesbury Press, 1943), pp. 86-87. Adapted.